REASONS

FOR

BECOMING A METHODIST.

By Rev. I. SMITH,

FOR SOME YEARS A MEMBER OF THE CLOSE-COMMUNION CALVINIST BAPTIST CHURCH.

INCLUDING

A BRIEF ACCOUNT OF THE AUTHOR'S RELIGIOUS EXPERIENCE UP TO THE TIME OF HIS BECOMING A METHODIST.

TWENTY-FIRST EDITION.

New-York:

PUBLISHED BY CARLTON & PORTER,

200 MULBERRY-STREET.

CONTENTS.

PREFACE.

THIS unpretending volume is designed, in the first place, to answer the question so frequently asked the writer, — "How came you to be a Methodist?" Secondly, it is intended to supply a place which is not filled by any other book, by presenting, at one view, and in a brief and comprehensive manner, the distinguishing features and excellences of Methodism, both in its doctrines and economy; and also some of the evidences of their Scriptural character and great efficiency. Nothing is more evident than the fact, that Methodism still suffers greatly from the ignorance that quite generally prevails in regard to the true character of its distinguishing doctrines and usages, as well as from the misrepresentations of its enemies. To aid in removing the former and refuting the latter is the design of this work.

Should any of our Baptist friends object to the title by which we have designated them, we would merely say, that our former worthy pastor, the most able and influential man in his Association, was accustomed to say, that he would be willing to have it written in large capitals on the front of his hat, "*Close-Communion Calvinistic Baptist.*" For his manly, Christian frankness in declaring his sentiments we respected him, and for his earnest piety we loved him while living, and cherish his memory since he has gone to his reward in heaven.

In submitting his manuscript to the press, the writer yields to the judgment of those in whose opinions he places great confidence.

May all be brought at last, however we may differ in opinion here, to join the general church above, is the humble, but earnest, prayer of the

AUTHOR.

REASONS
FOR
BECOMING A METHODIST.

CHAPTER I.

SKETCH OF RELIGIOUS EXPERIENCE.

AT the age of fifteen I received my first serious impressions in regard to my true condition, as a sinner before God; and while attending a series of meetings held in the Methodist Church in the neighborhood of my father's residence, I obtained the pardon of my sins, through the atonement of Christ. Had I, at that time, been brought under the watch-care of the Church, I think it would have saved me from that fearful state of backsliding into which I subsequently fell. But at that time my parents, though professedly pious, (and I doubt not really so at heart,) were neither of them members of any particular church; nor were any of the family save one sister, who was a member of the

Freewill Baptist Church in the adjoining town, where the family had attended meeting for some years. Having, therefore, no settled place of worship, and being left without the watch-care and restraining influences which every Christian church exercises over its members; and, also, being at a period of life when, above all others, I most needed them, I soon grew negligent of duty, sacrificed my peace of mind, indulged in the follies of youth, lost my confidence before the world, and in the presence of my Saviour refused to bear the cross, and "walked again in the counsel of the ungodly, stood in the way of sinners, and sat in the seat of the scornful." So hardened did I become in sin, that I approached to the very verge of infidelity; but, through the infinite mercy and compassion of the Redeemer, I was not left to make the dreadful plunge into the dark abyss. To this day, when I reflect upon my situation at that time, I shudder at the thought of my near approach to the pit of destruction, and can never feel sufficiently grateful to God for my happy deliverance through grace.

When about eighteen years of age I was

partially reclaimed from my backslidings, but still neglecting my duty to confess Christ before the world, and identify myself with the people of God, I soon relapsed in a measure, though never, I think, to the extent in sin to which I had previously gone. I was far, however, from living the life of a Christian. At this time I sincerely endeavored to persuade myself that Universalism was true; I read several books advocating this doctrine, went to hear ministers of this order preach; but I soon found that in exact proportion to my interest and confidence in their sentiments, was my entire indifference to all experimental godliness; and also that their sentiments were directly at war with the entire Scriptures.

At the age of twenty God was pleased to call after me again, in a special manner, during a revival of religion in the town where I resided, and at that time I fully resolved to devote myself to the service of God, and no more trample upon his mercy and grace. This resolution I have been enabled by his grace, in some good degree, I trust, to keep until this time, and I still have a strong confidence that I shall, by the same grace, be enabled to continue in his service to the end of life. At that time my oldest brother and wife were members of the close-communion Calvinist Baptist Church; the only members of the family then living, (the sister referred to having died in peace some years before,) connected with any church. I subsequently united with the same church, though not until some months had passed, and I had read to some extent on the subject of baptism, &c. I do not however recollect of having seen a single book in defence of the views of the Pedo-Baptists; for such works were not as abundant and accessible in that vicinity, as those in favor of the exclusive views of the Baptists; neither do I recollect ever hearing a sermon on the subject of baptism up to that time, or for some years after, except those preached by Baptists. The latter, however, were neither few nor far between. I am confident that my experience, in this particular, is not unlike most others. The truth is, that nearly all that is said on the subject of baptism, is said by Baptists, and of course all or one side.

I remained a member of that church about three years. During that time I was strongly urged by a celebrated Baptist evangelist, who held a protracted meeting in the church, to enter the ministry, but I had not then any expectations of ever filling so responsible an office.

I felt it, however, my duty to be more active in the cause of religion than I had hitherto been. With this conviction I went West, intending to teach, an occupation I had followed during the winter seasons for several years. I hoped by this means to enlarge my field of usefulness, in thus placing myself in direct communication with the rising generation — one of the most hopeful fields of Christian effort.

While engaged in teaching in Ohio I providentially fell in with President Mahan's Lectures on Christian Perfection, and was greatly interested in that (to me) new subject. About this time I became deeply impressed by the Spirit, and the leadings of Divine Providence, that it was my duty to preach the gospel. But to yield my mind to these convictions was a most difficult task. I pleaded my age, my want of preparation, and many other circumstances in excuse; still I felt that "woe is me if I preach not the Gospel." I often returned from the place of worship to weep and pray all night; sometimes waking from my sleep in distress, and sometimes dreaming of my duty. Finding no rest, I yielded to my convictions, and promised the Lord I would submit to his will.

Having closed my school I went to Oberlin, in the winter of 1841, and commenced my studies for the ministry. There my mind was still more deeply interested in the subject of Christian holiness, and more fully enlightened in regard to its *nature*, both by the preaching I heard, and the opportunity I had of associating with those who stood as living witnesses of its truth, confirming their testimony by their daily walk and conversation.

After much reflection and prayer, and as thorough an investigation of the Scriptures and other writings as I was able to make, I became fully satisfied that the doctrine was true. That what God requires, what the prophets, apostles, and the Saviour himself prayed for, and that what God has promised to give, might be obtained. That I — that every Christian might love God with *all* his heart, and his neighbor as himself; be made *perfect in* LOVE.

I commenced seeking to obtain so desirable a blessing as that of a pure heart, or, in the language of the pious psalmist, "a clean heart and a right spirit." I was attentive to all the spiritual opportunities that I enjoyed, but I was yet ignorant of many things in regard to the means of obtaining the blessing I desired; and, like the sinner oftentimes when seeking pardon, I was laboring to make myself better, to get ready to receive it, instead of carefully examining my heart, that I might know its deformity, and making, in the strength of grace, an entire consecration of all to God, for time and for eternity, in faith relying upon his promise and faithfulness, to accept, "and cleanse me from all unrighteousness." But the Lord was leading me by his Spirit and providence in a way I knew not. I continued thus for some months, during which I enjoyed the clearest evidence of my acceptance with God, and of his presence with me daily. But I saw clearly that it was his pleasure that I should live near the throne. I had not that strong faith I witnessed in others, and saw promised to all in the Bible. I found, in the hour of temptation, that there were enemies within, propensities to evil, rising up and combining their influence with the enemy from without, in order to bring me into captivity to the law of sin. These were only kept down by constant watching, while it was the will of God that they should be *cast out.* I had not that *perfect love* which I saw plainly that the Bible required. I felt a burning zeal to do good, but I felt most sensibly the imperfections of my armor.

While in this frame of mind I went one evening to a prayer meeting. The spirit of the Master was there, and at the close a fellow student, who was a backslider, taking me by the hand, said, "Brother S——, you must go with me to my room. I cannot live so." I saw that he was in great distress of mind, and without hesitation accompanied him to his room. He seemed at times almost in despair, yet constantly crying for mercy, and entreating me to pray for him. This I endeavored to do, but he found no comfort. It was there I saw and felt my want of faith; and I went from that room fully resolved never to rest until I obtained that faith which claims the promise, and which can be exercised only when "our heart condemns us not." Nothing less than that "perfect love that casteth out fear," could inspire me with that faith; and without it I was but poorly qualified to labor for the salvation of souls.

That night a most glorious revival of religion commenced in the Institution; one of the most powerful I ever witnessed. It pervaded the entire Institution, then composed of nearly six hundred students, and the appropriate number of officers and teachers. I entered into a solemn covenant with a fellow student, to spend all the time, save that necessary for sleep, our meals, and attending meeting, in earnest and united prayer for the attainment of the blessing we so earnestly desired, until our efforts should be crowned with success. Many were the hours we spent in our rooms, in the fields, and wherever we could find a retired spot, earnestly pleading for "a clean heart and a right spirit." Oftentimes we seemed almost to grasp the prize, when the tempter, taking advantage of our ignorance and inexperience, would divert our minds from Christ and his promise, to looking to our feelings, comparing our state of mind with others, &c., and by these means lead us again into darkness.

After having labored in this way about a week, we were enabled, through the counsels of one of the tutors in college, and the grace of God, to commit ourselves entirely upon the promise and faithfulness of God our Saviour, believing, according to the divine assurance, that he accepted in the present tense. And although this exercise of faith was not attended at the time with any particular emotions of joy, or any other than a consciousness of having given all for Christ, and of relying implicitly and unwaveringly on his promise to save to the uttermost, or from all sin, I at once felt a degree of confidence in prayer, a strength of faith I never realized before. I could pray directly to God through Christ. I seemed suspended by the single cord of God's love, revealed in his promise, holding on by the hand of faith, every prop, by way of works and every thing else, but the love of God in Christ, being removed from beneath me; and there I hung, perfectly safe, a sinner saved by grace, through faith. Satan buffeted me, but I held on as for my life; yea, for eternal life. I was fully resolved never to let go my hold of the promise, come joy or sorrow.

Having remained in this state of mind about twenty-four hours, I received such a baptism of the Spirit, as I had never before known or anticipated; my soul was filled with joy unspeakable and full of glory. It was enough; my heart was overflowing with love, peace, and joy in the Holy Ghost. Of the reality of my experience at this time I have no more doubt than I have of my personal existence. But it was all of grace, through faith; and to the honor of that grace, in the Saviour provided, and in the gospel promised, it ever has been and ever shall be declared.

Up to this time I had never had the least doubt of the correctness of my position as a close-communion Baptist. Indeed, so absorbed had I been in the pursuit of the ruling desire of my heart, that I had scarcely thought upon the subject at all. But a great change had taken place in my feelings toward the members of other churches. I had lost entirely, though almost insensibly, all those uncharitable feelings which are the natural and almost necessary result of holding and advocating the exclusive views of the Baptist Church. I found my confidence, love, and sympathy flowing out to members of other churches with the same ardor with which they were extended to members of the Baptist Church. I had come to love Christians in the ratio of their likeness to Christ, and not according to the name they bore.

About this time the sacrament of the Lord's Supper was administered in the church. It was a season of great interest; a deep solemnity pervaded the entire congregation. The people of God were greatly refreshed and humbled; backsliders were tremblingly alive to a sense of their ingratitude, and the impenitent were awed into a solemn reverence. All felt that God was there of a truth to bless and sanction his ordinance, and to comfort and sanctify his people in the performance of their most solemn duty. In accordance with my principles of close communion I sat one side, a silent looker on, but not an idle spectator; few, if any such, could be found in that large audience, for God was in the midst of them.

It was a combination of such circumstances and influences that first led me to question the correctness of my principles in regard to the communion. This being a Congregational Church, few if any of the members had ever been immersed, and they were, therefore, in my view, unbaptized, and had no right to come to the table of the Lord; and in truth, upon such principles there was no table of the Lord there, and no Church, and no *authorized* administrator of the sacrament. None of the persons having been baptized, they were none of them in the Church; as baptism is, according to the Baptists' doctrine, the only door into the Church; and as neither ministers nor members belonged to the Church, it was impossible for them to administer or receive her exclusive privileges. Yet many of those communicants I personally knew, and knew them to be deeply pious, to enjoy the presence, communion, and fellowship of God by his Spirit in an eminent degree; and I now perceived that the Lord not only owned and blessed them, as Christians, extending to them what a Baptist would call Christian fellowship, but that he owned and blessed them in a remarkable manner, in the *very act of administering and receiving the sacrament* — in administering and receiving that which my principles pronounced them without authority to administer, and unqualified to receive. I was as well satisfied that many, at least, of those persons were Christians, and enjoyed communion with God our Saviour, as I was that religion was to be found in the world. I was as sensible of the presence and blessing of God among the people at that sacrament, as I was that God ever owns and blesses his children.

I began to inquire into the propriety of my being more particular and exclusive in *my fellowship* than my Master! I reasoned thus: — If God owns, blesses, and communes with them at the sacrament, why should I refuse to participate with them in the blessings of our common Lord and Saviour? Many of them I knew enjoyed much more of God's presence and grace than myself, and if the mere fact that they had not been baptized according to the decisions of my fallible judgment, was a good reason why I should admonish them, by withholding my fellowship, why did not the Lord, the Great Teacher and Master in Israel, withhold his blessing, and rebuke them, by refusing to commune with them? He declares himself a God jealous of his honor. Was I to be more jealous than he? Was I more holy, or was my sanction more dangerous? These reflections led me to my Bible — to carefully examine and review this whole subject. For most surely, thought I, nothing less than the most *positive scriptural authority*, can justify a practice so inconsistent with every noble, generous, Christian feeling or sentiment, as is that of close-communion. But after a careful examination of the Scriptures, and much prayer, I came to the settled conviction, that the Scriptures nowhere authorize us to exclude all unbaptized, much less all unimmersed persons from the sacrament of the Lord's Supper. That although it is desirable as a matter of order, that baptism should precede the Lord's Supper, yet I am fully satisfied that there is no authority in the Bible for making it a universal rule. There plainly, both from reason and the Scriptures, must be many exceptions. The proof of this, if any be needed, I shall have occasion to present hereafter.

But although the principle was established in my mind, yet the most difficult and unpleasant task remained. A greater cross was yet to be borne — to make known my views to my old friends, and especially to my brother, whom I loved as Jonathan loved David, and whom I knew to be a strong Baptist. I feared the loss of his warm friendship, knowing very well that persons who for any cause left the Baptist Church were regarded with any other than a friendly feeling. I hesitated for a time, but finally yielded to my convictions of duty, and communicated to him my views on the subject of the communion, and was not a little surprised to learn from him that his mind had undergone the same change, and that he had been afflicted with similar apprehensions of losing that ardent affection and sympathy which had hitherto existed between us.

On the subject of Calvinism my mind had

never been fully settled, although I had been enabled to assent to it, so far as was necessary to be received into the Baptist Church. But the more I heard and studied upon the subject, the more I was convinced that it was dangerous in its tendency, and contrary to the experience and common sense of all men, and without foundation in the Scriptures. About this time my health failing me, I returned to the East, to my native town.

Here I must be allowed to digress from my main purpose, to pay a tribute of respect to an institution and a class of Christians, whom I have every reason to esteem, both for their faith and practice. Though I do not embrace every sentiment held and advocated by them, I can most cheerfully say, that during my stay at Oberlin I witnessed, both in the institution and among the people generally, as much deep and practical piety as I have ever seen among any people whatever. And I think if those who have spent so much time in endeavoring to overthrow their sentiments, would have labored more to imitate their earnest piety, it would have been much better for them and for the world at large. The Lord bless the brethren at Oberlin, has ever been the language of my heart since I made their acquaintance. I have been greatly benefited by their writings and their preaching, as well as by their godly examples.

No longer satisfied with being confined in my sympathies and fellowship to the limits of the Baptist Church; believing it also my duty, as well as privilege, to extend the hand of fellowship to all God's children, members of the household of faith; and no longer believing the doctrines of Calvinism, and regarding it as highly improper to practice or profess, what I did not believe, I went before the church and stated to them my views on communion, and my intention of putting them in practice. This I had not yet done, nor did I feel at liberty to do so until I had made my position known to the church. Whereupon the church voted to withdraw fellowship from me, on the account of my heretical sentiments in regard to the communion. But finally it was concluded, as a matter of policy, to withdraw that action, and wait till I had violated some rule of the church, at the same time expressing an unwillingness to receive me at their table. The next day being the Sabbath, I received the sacrament in the Congregational Church, and a short time after I had the privilege of communing in the Methodist Church, and I could not perceive but that I was as much profited and blessed as I ever had been when communing with my Baptist brethren. A committee was very soon appointed by the church to visit and labor with me on this account, and I was notified to appear before the church for trial, on charge of embracing and practicing open-communion principles. The appointed day arrived, and I presented myself, with Bible in hand, to see the end and abide the consequences. During the trial it was distinctly and repeatedly declared, by the elder, deacons, and others, that they had nothing against me except my principles and practice in regard to the communion; that as a Christian they fellowshipped me, and as cordially extended to me the hand of *Christian fellowship* as they ever did; but they could not extend to me the hand of *Church fellowship*, because I did nct walk orderly. There was a great difference, they said, between *Christian* and *Church* fellowship; the first they still had for me, but not the latter.

I urged, in my defence, the absence of any Scriptural authority for excluding from the Supper all unbaptized persons, or any true Christian; that the Scriptures represented all true Christians as one in Christ, members of his body, and entitled to the same privileges; that the examples left on record by the apostles, of church discipline, were either in cases of immorality, or a wilful neglect of a plain duty, or a perversion of the fundamental principles of the Gospel, thereby endangering the salvation of souls; that the New Testament drew the line of distinction between saints and sinners—those who obeyed and those who disobeyed, those who loved God, and those who loved him not, but nowhere between the baptized and the unbaptized; and finally, that many good Christians, holy men and eminent for talent, who had studied the Bible prayerfully to know their duty, as sincerely believed they had been validly baptized by sprinkling, as they did that they had been by immersion. Although I was not prepared, at that time, to advocate their views of baptism, yet if the Lord was so far satisfied with their baptism as not only to commune with them by his Spirit, but to own and bless them in the act of partaking of the Supper, which he evidently did in an especial manner, I could no longer refuse to give them my hand in fellowship. Those that were good enough for the Lord to fellowship were good enough for me. I dared not claim to be either better or wiser than my Master. Whom the Lord received, I received. Those He fellowshipped, I must fellowship.

The church then proceeded, without making any reply to my positions, (though an elder said they could be answered without any trouble,) to vote upon the question of expulsion, and I was declared expelled from the church. The question being decided, I requested the church to give me a letter, recommending me to the *Christian* fellowship of the Lord's people, wherever my lot might be cast. Some objections being made, such as want of precedent, &c., I gave them these reasons for making the request: I was expecting to go immediately among entire strangers, and should in all probability go before uniting with any church, and I might be placed in circumstances where the fact of my having been turned out of the church would prove a serious embarrassment to me, and where a letter of the kind I suggested would not only prevent any such difficulty, but also give me an introduction to the Lord's children.

My second reason was, I wished to test the truth of a sentiment prevailing among all Baptists, and which they had so frequently avowed during the trial, viz., that they had *Christian* fellowship for me and others, for whom they could not have CHURCH fellowship. If they had it, as they said, I wished them to put it in black and white, and show that it was a *reality*, and not mere talk. But they refused to do it, thereby proving to a demonstration the correctness of an opinion I had entertained, and in which I have since been confirmed, viz., that their distinction between *Christian* and *Church* fellowship is a distinction without a difference; and that just in proportion to their confidence in, and zeal for, their exclusive views of baptism and the communion, will be found their want of charity for, and sympathy with, all who think differently from themselves in this matter — or are not Baptists.* That the course pursued in my case is in accordance with their general practice, may be seen from the fact that an influential Baptist Church recently expelled one of her oldest members, on the charge of *heresy*, for merely holding the opinion that it was her privilege to commune with other Christians besides Baptists, though she had never even expressed the *intention* of doing it. Elder M., a popular preacher, and one of their strong men, was asked this question: "Do you believe that any who are not immersed will be saved?" He evaded a direct reply; but being pressed to answer, he said in substance, if not in these very words, "I do not profess to be wise above what is written. The Bible says none will be saved who do not obey the gospel. And none obey the gospel, who are not immersed."

* The clerk of the church subsequently gave me a certified copy of the record of my connection with the church, and stating that at such a time I embraced and practiced open-communion principles, "and for this and *this only* I was labored with, and cut off from the church."

That Baptists do at times, and in some individual instances habitually, have charity for and fellowship with other denominations, is evident. But it is only when they lay aside their views on baptism and the communion, for the time, and give their attention to the great and fundamental principles of the gospel, laboring to save souls. While they have this fellowship in exercise they would gladly commune with all God's children but for the *rule*, and when the *spirit* of *Church* fellowship disappears, we look in vain for *Christian* fellowship. Where one exists, the other is sure to be found, and when one ceases, the other ceases also. The moment you touch the subject of baptism, every zealous Baptist invariably loses all his Christian fellowship. Who has not seen an exhibition of these things in a revival? It is indeed inconsistent with their principles for them to recognize any other church or ministry than their own. For, according to their views of baptism, and its relation to the church, there can be no other church or ministry. Their principles are no less exclusive and bigoted than the High Churchman's and the Romanist's. And the fact that they utterly refuse to give their members letters to any other church save a Baptist, proves conclusively that they so regard it.

A man who had belonged to the Methodist Church became a Baptist; he was asked if he had called for a letter, or said any thing to them of his intention of leaving? He replied: "No, nor do I intend to, for I do not consider that they have any church, or any right to give a letter." This he had learned in his new school, and it is in perfect keeping with their general practice; though they are generally careful to tell it as *publicly as possible* after they have fairly secured one from another fold! But it is inquired, if they hold such sentiments why do their ministers exchange with other denominations, thereby virtually recognizing their ministry and church membership? We answer, it is, in many instances, because their religion predominates over their exclusive sentiments, while in others it is undoubtedly a mere matter of policy. It would be any thing but popular, or policy, for them to refuse such intercourse. It would be obnoxious to the sentiments of Christian people generally. But we are well aware that many who belong to the Baptist Church have no sympathy for these bigoted sentiments. But being in favor of immersion, they have joined the Baptists as *one branch* of Christ's Church, not considering the exclusive character of their sentiments; while others saw, and revolted at first at the thought of their excluding from their fellowship all other Christians, and adopting such narrow and big oted sentiments. But believing that immersion is the only mode of baptism, and assuming as true what they were falsely told by Baptists, that all denominations believed, viz., that no person, however pious, ought to come to the communion if he had not been baptized, they have, though reluctantly, embraced these sentiments in view of all their necessary conclusions, and set themselves to defend them. As a natural consequence, they soon find their feelings in agreement with the exclusiveness of their sentiments, which, as we have seen, are nearly allied to the intolerance of Romanism, as says their great apostle, Rev. Robert Hall, himself a Baptist, but rejecting close communion. "I am fully persuaded," he says, "that few of our brethren have duly reflected on the strong resemblance which subsists between the pretensions of the Church of Rome and the principles implied in strict communion; *both equally intolerant;* the one armed with pains and penalties, the other, I trust, disdaining such aid: the one the intolerance of power, the other of weakness." He also says in another place, that "the close-communion Baptists make the door into their church narrower than the gate to Heaven."

CHAPTER II.

COMPREHENSIVE VIEW OF THE DOCTRINES OF THE M. E. CHURCH.

BEING now fully separated from the Baptist Church, and believing it my duty, as well as privilege, to belong to and enjoy the spiritual aids of some branch of Christ's Church, I began carefully to examine the doctrines and usages of the different evangelical communions. Having no prepossessions in favor of any one in particular, I trusted, with divine assistance, that I might form at least an *impartial judgment* in my choice. But I would not intimate that others had not been as impartial in their choice, and yet chosen differently. I shall endeavor to give, as briefly as possible, the reason for preferring the Methodist Episcopal Church, without reflecting in the least on those who are of a different opinion.

Three things demand the prayerful consideration of every person in determining with what branch of the Christian church he shall unite — viz., purity and simplicity of doctrine, the means afforded for spiritual improvement, and facilities for doing good, or of fulfilling the great design and commission of the church, to convert the world. After about six months' diligent and prayerful investigation, and in view of these considerations, I deliberately, and from a solemn conviction of duty, united with the M. E. Church, because I sincerely believed her doctrines to be purer, more like the simplicity of the gospel, and in greater harmony with each other; that her usages afforded better opportunities for my spiritual improvement and growth in grace, also greater advantages for doing good, than any of the other churches with which I was acquainted. My reasons for this opinion will be found in the following brief statement of some of the most important doctrines and usages of Methodism.

Methodists hold, in common with other evangelical churches, the doctrine of the Trinity, the depravity of man's nature, the vicarious atonement of Christ, the immortality of the soul, and a future state of everlasting rewards and punishments. They believe that man was created holy, "in the image of God," possessing the power of choice, or the ability to choose between good and evil; that he did, of his own free will, choose evil, thereby incurring the penalty which God had denounced against him in case of such disobedience. This was *death.* "In the day thou eatest thereof thou shalt surely die." They believe on that day he died; his body became as dead in the eyes of the law; for its sentence was pronounced against him, "Dust thou art, and unto the dust shalt thou return;" and he at once entered into a state of spiritual death, losing God's image from his heart, which consisted in "righteousness and true holiness." In this state of *death,* both body and soul were involved; all ability to do good was lost, and man would have been for ever dead in sin, (and consequently the whole prospective race in him;) for this must of necessity have remained to all eternity, unless it can be shown that death will sometime bring forth life. This must have been the end of the race, but for the promise of a Redeemer, "the seed of the woman." Through this gracious provision, there was secured to man another state of probation, in which he might regain what he had lost by sin, viz., the image and favor of God. This provision, or the atonement of Christ, is an unconditional and universal remedy for sinful man. He was "a Lamb slain from the foundation of the world," "not for our sins only, but for the sins of the *whole world*." The benefits of the atonement are in part unconditional, and in part conditional. Among the unconditional benefits we notice the resurrection of the body, "both of the just and of the unjust;" the removing of the guilt of original sin, so that we are not held accountable for it; and restoring to man the ability to turn from his sins and seek the grace and mercy of God, through Christ — "that grace of God which bringeth salvation (and) hath appeared to all men," "that *light* which lighteth every man that cometh into the world." Among the conditional benefits of the atonement are the pardon of our sins, the renewing or regeneration of our hearts by the Holy Ghost, the sanctification of our spirits; in short the present and eternal salvation of our souls is offered to us on condition of our faith in Christ; that we repent of our sins, believe on the Lord Jesus Christ, and bring forth the fruits of obedience. Hence we believe "in God the Saviour of all men, (and) the special Saviour of them that believe." "That Christ gave himself a *ransom for all*," yet "he that believeth not *shall be damned*."

These views of the atonement, though adopted by some others, are nevertheless peculiarities of Methodism, distinguishing it from the doctrine of the high Calvinists, who hold that Christ died only for the elect. Methodists believe, in accordance with the whole tenor of the Scriptures, that life and salvation are freely offered to every man, and that God gives to every intelligent, accountable being, grace sufficient to enable him to receive the offer of life and be saved, and then calls upon every individual to choose for himself whom he will serve; persuading and entreating him to choose life, but leaving him free to choose death. They believe that God never did, and never will bring any irresistible influences to bear upon any person, to insure their salvation,* but that there is one universal offer and invitation made to *all*, which all are alike free to accept, and all alike free to reject. With propriety, then, may God say, "Are not my ways equal?" And Paul may assert that "He is no respecter of persons," a God "without partiality."

Thus does Methodism give all the praise and glory of man's salvation to God's grace, while it casts all the blame of the sinner's neglect and consequent destruction upon himself. They might have come but they "*would not.*" "They knew their duty but did it not." In this, the Methodist Church differs materially from all Calvinistic churches; from the old school Calvinists, who hold with Calvin that God decreed from all eternity whom he would save, without any regard to their faith or obedience, and, also, whom he would damn, without any regard to their unbelief and disobedience," and that "the number of the elect, and also of the reprobates,

* The case of Saul is said to be an instance of irresistible conversion. But he was miraculously convicted of the truth of Christianity, and no farther, for he says, "*I was not disobedient to the heavenly vision*," showing that obedience was wholly voluntary on his part.

was so definitely fixed that it could not be increased or diminished." No wonder Calvin called it "*a horrible decree.*" Yet most Calvinists in past ages have believed it; in some form or other it is found in their creeds. They differ no less in reality, though some less in appearance, from the modern Calvinists, who hold that God has foreordained whatsoever comes to pass; so that not only nothing comes to pass without his knowledge and permission, but "not without his foreordaining it," sin not excepted. Also they teach that God gives to all men common grace, or a common call which none ever obey, and which they have not the moral power necessary to obey; and then that he gives to the elect a special call, or effectual grace, as they term it, and all such will necessarily be brought in, by a kind of irresistible influence. Those that receive the *special* call, they teach, are no less sinful and ill-deserving than others who only have a *common* call. I once asked a Calvinist minister if he believed that if God had been pleased to give the same grace to those who are now in hell, that he did give unconditionally to those who are in heaven, that they would have been saved? He replied, "I have no doubt but they would." How then can he be what Paul declares him to be, "a God without partiality," and "no respecter of persons?" Are such "*ways equal?*" Is it said, he was under no obligation to any? That does not help the matter in the least. If a man had three sons, all equally unworthy, and equally needy, and should bestow large favors upon two, and none on the other, would he not be partial? And how can God punish men eternally for not obeying the gospel, when they never had the power to obey it? Is it said that their wicked hearts are all that render it morally impossible for them to obey? But did they not bring those very wicked hearts into the world with them? and have they ever had the power or grace necessary to change them, on their own principles? If not, are they in fault? Some, pressed with these monstrous absurdities, have taken the opposite extreme, and deny the doctrine of depravity, and assert that man has a natural ability, independent of the Spirit or grace of God, to change his heart, and live a holy life. So one extreme begets its opposite.

Who can help admiring the simplicity and consistency of Methodism, especially when contrasted with these *mysteries mystified?* We confess it looks to us like a beautiful and harmonious system of gospel truth.

But it is said, Calvinist ministers preach free salvation, free grace, and free will, as well as Methodists! This reminds me of the remarks of a worthy and influential Baptist minister, who was unusually frank and outspoken in all his sentiments, for which we respect and honor him. "They say," said he, "that Elder B—— preaches election and predestination in the morning, and free will and free salvation in the afternoon, and that one contradicts the other. Well, I find (Calvinian) election and predestination in the Bible, and I preach it; I find free will and free salvation in the Bible, and I preach it; it is not my business to reconcile the Scriptures, but to preach them!" This was a most commendable acknowledgment, viz., that Calvinian election and free salvation are irreconcilable.

Methodists believe it the privilege of every Christian to enjoy the witness of the Spirit to have, "the Spirit witnessing with their spirits that they are born of God." That they may *know* their acceptance with God, having the witness in their hearts crying Abba Father; and be able to say with the Apostle John, "And hereby we know that he abideth in us, by the Spirit which he hath given us." This is one of the peculiarities of Methodism; and although it is at the present day admitted, and sometimes advocated, by others, yet it should be remembered that within fifty years, yea a much less time, Methodists were regarded and represented as a band of wild *fanatics*, who pretended to know their acceptance with God; and were accused by all Calvinist churches of boasting of their piety, being self-righteous because they preached and professed to enjoy the witness of the Spirit. These contended that no one could know whether he was a Christian or not; he might have *a faint hope;* but he must wait in uncertainty till after death, or until the Judgment; and then, if he was one of the elect, well; if not, his hopes would perish; that just in proportion to a person's confidence that he had religion, was the probability that he was deceived, and if he knew he had it, he was certainly without it. But we are thankful that a better sentiment is prevailing at the present day, and we hope to see the leaven work until the whole lump is leavened. Let it not, however, be forgotten that the Methodists were the first in modern times to advocate the doctrine that we might know our acceptance with God, and that they did it at the sacrifice of their reputation among other denominations. Who would wish to travel all his days in a state of awful uncertainty, not knowing whether he was going in the way to Heaven or direct to hell? No wonder that those who believed this considered religion a gloomy subject, an *awful mystery;* but "I show unto you a more excellent way."

The doctrine of Christian perfection, or holiness of heart, is another distinguishing doctrine of Methodism, and one that first drew my attention to it. There is, to me, and to every true Methodist, a peculiar excellence and importance in the doctrine of perfect love; and it is a great privilege to sit under the preaching of those who not only teach, but live in the enjoyment of this blessing; and especially to be a fellow laborer with them in such a work; viz., "in spreading scriptural holiness over these lands." A work delightful to perform, and glorious to contemplate.

Methodists do not believe in any absolute perfection. They believe that men will of necessity be imperfect in many things. They must be imperfect in knowledge, and consequently liable to many mistakes, both in thought and action. But God judgeth the heart — the motive — and that being pure, he accepts, and imputes to us no sin, though our acts be imperfect, and even sinful in themselves, provided we improve all the means we have to gain light and a knowledge of our duty. They believe that men, while in the body, will be liable to sin, and subject to temptation; for they read that "Christ was tempted, yet without sin." But they believe that it is the privilege of all to secure the blessing promised by Christ to "the pure in heart;" that they may with David pray for a "clean heart and a right spirit," expecting to receive it; that they may be made perfect in love — loving God with *all the heart*, and their neighbor *as themselves*, as God requires, and that they may pray with Paul, (not in unbelief, but in faith, nothing wavering,) that "the very God of peace (would) sanctify (them) wholly, and preserve (them) blameless unto the coming of our Lord and Saviour Jesus Christ."

Methodists believe it the privilege of all Christians to enjoy the blessing of holiness, or perfect love, in this life, for the following reasons: 1st. God is infinitely benevolent, and wills or desires for man the highest possible degree of happiness. But man can only enjoy such happiness when he is holy, or freed from his enemy, sin, and restored to the image of God, which consists "in righteousness and true holiness." 2d. Salvation has God for its author, Jesus Christ its sacrifice for sin, the Holy Ghost its sanctifier; and who dare say, that a salvation provided by the combined efforts of the whole Trinity will still be insufficient to save from all sin? that the infinitely wise and holy Redeemer has undertaken to save man, and has failed to provide for him a complete or perfect salvation from sin? 3d. The word of God requires it. "Thou shalt love the Lord thy God with all thy heart, and thy neighhor as thyself."

"Be ye holy, for I the Lord your God am holy." "Be ye therefore perfect, even as your Father which is in Heaven is perfect." The connection shows this to be a perfection in *love*, that is required. They do not believe that God requires more of man than his grace will enable him to perform; for he says, "it is required according to what a man hath, and not according to what he hath not." 4th. But as much holiness is promised through Christ as is required by his word: "And the Lord thy God shall circumcise thy heart, that thou *mayest love* the Lord thy God with *all thy heart.*" "Then will I sprinkle clean water upon you, and ye shall be clean; from *all* your filthiness and from *all* your idols will I cleanse you. A new heart also will I give you, and a new spirit will I put within you: and I will take away the stony heart out of your flesh, and I will give you a heart of flesh. And I will put my Spirit within you, and cause you to walk in my statutes, and ye shall keep my judgments, and do them." "And the blood of Jesus Christ his Son cleanseth us from all sin." Again, "If we confess our sins, he is faithful and just, to forgive us our sins, *and to cleanse us from all unrighteousness.*" And the apostle declares that it was for this very purpose, viz., that he might sanctify his people, that the Saviour gave himself a ransom for our sins; "as Christ also loved the church, and gave himself for it, *that he might sanctify and cleanse it* with the washing of water by the word. That he might present it to himself, a glorious church, not having *spot* or *wrinkle*, or *any such thing;* but that it should be *holy and without blemish.*" * 5th. For this the Saviour, the apostles, and the prophets prayed. The Saviour, in his last prayer on earth, prayed for his disciples, saying, "Sanctify them through thy truth, thy word is truth." Paul prayed in behalf of the Thessalonians: "May the very God of peace sanctify you wholly; and I pray God your whole spirit, and soul, and body be preserved blameless, unto (not after) the coming of our Lord and Saviour Jesus Christ." The apostle here prays for the blessing of entire sanctification in this life in the most positive terms, and then adds, "Faithful is he that call-

*Isa. i. 18, 25; Jer. xxxiii. 8; Ps. lxxiii. 1; cxix. 186; Titus ii. 14; 1 John iv. 16—18.

eth you, who also *will do it.*" In his letter to the Ephesians, he says: "For this cause I bow my knees unto the Father of our Lord Jesus Christ, of whom the whole family in heaven and earth is named, that he would grant you, according to the riches of his glory, to be strengthened with might by his Spirit in the inner man; that Christ may dwell in your hearts by faith; that ye, being rooted and grounded in love, may be able to comprehend *with all saints* what is the breadth, and length, and depth, and height; and to know the love of Christ, which passeth knowledge, that ye might be filled with all the fulness of God. Now unto him that is able to do exceeding abundantly above all that we ask or think, according to the power that worketh in us, unto him be glory in the Church by Christ Jesus, throughout all ages, world without end. Amen." In his epistle to the Hebrews he says: "Now the God of peace, that brought again from the dead our Lord Jesus, that great Shepherd of the sheep, through the blood of the everlasting covenant, make you *perfect in every good work to do his will*, working in you that which is well-pleasing in his sight, through Jesus

Christ; to whom be glory for ever and ever. Amen." * Now who will dare say, that the Saviour, or that Paul did not pray in faith, or that their prayers were never answered? 6th. The apostles and many of the early Christians enjoyed it. Paul says, "The law of the spirit of life in Christ Jesus hath made me free from the law of sin and death." "I am crucified with Christ, nevertheless I live; yet not I, but Christ liveth in me." And again, "Ye are witnesses, and God also, how *holily* and *justly* and unblamably we behaved ourselves among you that believe." † A cloud of witnesses have arisen up in the church who have borne witness to the truth of this doctrine; both testifying with their lips, to the glory of God's grace, and showing by their godly lives, that the blood of Christ cleansed them from all sin. They have lived rejoicing in a "*free* and *full* salvation," and when called to die, they have departed in the triumphs of faith, leaving their dying testimony in favor of the truth and blessedness of this doctrine of holiness. "Every man that

* Matt. vi. 10; Ps. li. 2, 7, 10.

† Job i 1; Luke i. 6; Phil. iii. 15; Ps. xxxvii. 37; Matt. v. 8.

hath this hope in him, purifieth himself even as he is pure." This is the doctrine of Methodism, in distinction from other denominations, who make the seventh of Romans the standard of Christian attainments. In this chapter Paul is evidently describing the state of the convicted Jew, seeking in vain for justification by the deeds of the law, in distinction from the grace of the gospel. No language can be found more fitly and fully to describe the state of the unregenerate, unbelieving heart, than that used by the apostle in the fourteenth verse of this chapter, viz., "*I am carnal,* SOLD UNDER SIN." There is not a passage in the Bible which represents the condition of the sinner as more wretched and lost than this. How unlike Paul the Christian, in the following chapter: "There is, therefore, now no condemnation to them which are in Christ Jesus, who walk not after the flesh, but after the Spirit. For the law of the spirit of life in Christ Jesus *hath made me free from the law of sin and death.*" He then gives the reason: "For what the law *could not do,* in that it was weak through the flesh, God sending *his own Son* in the likeness of sinful flesh, and for sin, *condemned sin in the flesh. That the righteousness of the law might be fulfilled in us, who walk not after the flesh but after the Spirit.*" But it is said by the opposers of this doctrine, that no man lives a single moment without being guilty of sin. Now what more, we ask, can the veriest sinner do, than sin every moment? But it is said, "the Bible says," that "no man liveth and sinneth not!" The Bible nowhere says this, but it does say that "There is no man that sinneth not." And the Apostle John has repeated the same sentiment, saying, "if we say we have no sin we deceive ourselves;" and he has explained both in the same chapter in which the last is found, saying, "If we say *we have not sinned*, we make him a liar, and the truth is not in us." That is, if we say we have no sins to be forgiven, no need of pardon, we deceive ourselves, and make him a liar who has declared that "all have sinned and come short of the glory of God."

Thus, while they are leaning upon this broken reed as an excuse for living in sin, and mourning over their barrenness, the Methodist is exclaiming with glorious hope, "If we confess our sins he is faithful and just to forgive us our sins, *and to cleanse us from all unrighteousness*;" or with the same apostle, declaring in triumph, and to the glory of God's grace, "The blood of Jesus Christ his Son, cleanseth us *from all sin*." Who can hesitate as to which of these doctrines he shall embrace, when he considers, either the authority on which they rest, or the nature of the doctrines themselves? Which is best adapted to the wants of men? which best accords with the character of the divine Author of salvation, in whom dwelt all the fulness of the Godhead bodily? Would he undertake to save man, to make provision for his salvation, and leave the work imperfect, to be completed by death or some other agency? No! no! we have a perfect Saviour, a perfect atonement for sin, a perfect salvation provided for the souls of men, and offered to us in the present tense, without money and without price.

But while Methodists believe it to be the privilege of all to enjoy that "holiness without which no man shall see the Lord," they believe, and constantly teach, that it is all of grace, free, unmerited grace, *through faith* in Christ Jesus.

They believe also that it can only be retained by a continual exercise of the same grace, the grace of "faith that *works by love*." They continually proclaim to all, "Let him that standeth take heed lest he fall!" "For the just shall *live* by faith," as well as be justified and sanctified by faith.

They believe, also, that it is possible for the Christian to fall from any degree of grace to which he may attain in this world, and so fall as to be finally lost, or "be a castaway." In this they differ from all Calvinists, who hold the doctrine that "once in grace, always in grace," or that a person once converted is as sure of heaven as the glorified saints on high. But Methodists believe that Christians may fall, because they are yet in a state of probation, which could not be, if there was no possibility of their being lost.

The Christian lives by faith, and faith is a voluntary exercise of mind, — that is, the act of believing. The power to believe is the gift of God, but the exercise of that power or gracious ability is a voluntary act of ours; and as the Christian may cease to believe, so he may cease to live spiritually, and dying in this state of unbelief and disobedience, as he is certainly liable to, he is as sure to be lost as any other unbeliever. But "no!" said a Baptist minister; "God will never suffer a backslider to die in that state." Now if this is true, all a backslider has to do in order to live for ever, is to take care not to be reclaimed. An army of such would conquer the world, for powder and lead could not touch them.

But the Bible expressly says there is danger, and in every part its warning voice is raised, admonishing us to beware lest we fall. The Scriptures tell us of the angels "who kept not their first estate," but fell from their high and holy position; of Adam and Eve, who fell in Paradise; and the apostles point us to the case of the rebellious Jews, who fell in the wilderness, saying, "Moreover, brethren, I would not that ye should be ignorant, how that *all* our fathers were under the cloud, and all passed through the sea, and were all baptized unto Moses in the cloud, and in the sea; and did all eat the same spiritual meat; and did all drink the same spiritual drink; for they drank of that spiritual rock that followed them: *and that Rock was Christ.* But with many of them God was not well pleased; for they were overthrown in the wilderness. Now these things were our examples, *to the intent* we should not lust after evil things, as they also lusted. Now all these things happened unto them for *ensamples (or types:) and they are written for our admonition*, upon whom the ends of the world are come. Wherefore let him that thinketh he standeth *take heed lest he fall.*" He that never stood, could never be in *danger* of falling. The Evangelists tell us of Judas, one of the twelve, "who by transgression fell from his apostleship, and went and hanged himself." Ezekiel says, "When a righteous man turneth away from his righteousness, and committeth iniquity, *and dieth in them*, for his iniquity that he hath done shall he *die.* All his righteousness that he hath done shall not be mentioned: in his trespass that he hath trespassed, and in his sin that he hath sinned, in them shall he die." And this is not, as has been said, a righteousness by the law, and not of Grace; for it is added, "Again, when the wicked man turneth away from his wickedness that he hath committed, and doeth that which is lawful and right, he shall save his *soul alive.*" Now the law never pardons, but here is pardon promised, therefore it is of grace, and not a righteousness by the law. The Saviour says, "If a man abide not in me, he is cast forth as a branch, and is withered; and men gather them, and cast them into the fire and they are burned." Paul writing to Timothy speaks of some who "concerning faith have made shipwreck:" of others, as "having damnation, because they have *cast off their first faith.*" And to the Hebrews he says, "For it is impossible for those who were once enlightened, and have tasted of the heavenly gift, and were made partakers of the Holy Ghost, and have tasted the good Word of God, and the powers of the world to come, if they shall fall away, (or falling away, as the original has it,) to renew them again to repentance, seeing they crucify the Son of God afresh, and put him to an open shame." The persons here spoken of are evidently those who have been converted, and made partakers of the high privileges of the gospel, and have apostatized from Christianity, of whom there is no hope, seeing they reject the only Saviour. Again, "If we sin wilfully after that we have received the knowledge of the truth, there remaineth no more sacrifice for sin," &c. And again, "The just shall live by faith; but if any man draw back, my soul shall have no pleasure in him." And the apostle says of himself, "But I keep under my body, and bring it into subjection; lest that by any means, when I have preached to others, I myself should be a castaway." Peter also says, "Brethren, give diligence to make your calling and election sure, for *if ye do these things* (see the context preceding) ye shall never fall." Here are those called and elected, yet their calling and election can only be made *finally sure*, by their continuing in faithful obedience. To say there is no real danger of a Christian's falling, in view of these Scriptures, is to charge God with endeavoring to frighten his children when there is no danger or harm to be feared. Who, in the face of these facts and Scriptures, dare say that no person once a Christian will ever be lost? Is it not a pity, that when men are so prone to backsliding, that they should be encouraged in it, by being told there is no danger, "once in, always in." And, as I heard a Baptist minister say, in preaching on this subject, that "He believed that Christians in a backslidden state often glorified God as much as when heartily engaged in religion, for at such times they showed their decision and principle." And why not, if they are only carrying out God's will or decree? What is this but encouraging men to backslide? But, it is replied, no man can know, for a certainty, whether he is "in," or a Christian, and therefore if he backslides it is an evidence that he has been deceived. But this is a positive denial of the Scriptural doctrine of the "witness of the Spirit." To such miserable shifts does Calvinism drive its advocates. How unlike the simplicity of the gospel, which is so plain "that he may run that readeth it," "and the wayfaring men, though fools, shall not err therein."

Nothing is more evident to us, than that the direct tendency of the whole system of Calvinism, of which this is a part, is to confuse and bewilder the mind of the serious inquirer after truth; that it greatly weakens, and tends to destroy all sense of personal responsibility in the minds of both saint and sinner. The sinner very naturally reasons, "If I am to be saved, or to have an effectual call, I shall be brought in, as all who have it are; and if not, then it is of no use to try; for none without it ever were or ever will be saved; and as this grace is wholly unconditional, or given to whom He will, I may as well wait till it comes, if indeed it is to come at all. The Christian stands on the same ground, believing there is no danger — "once in, always in." It greatly hinders the zeal and faithfulness of Christians; and tends directly to the doctrine of fatality, and consequently to Universalism and open infidelity. This statement is not only confirmed by the history of a multitude of individuals, who have been driven by the ultra opinions of Calvinism into Unitarianism, Universalism, and in many instances to open infidelity; but the religious history of New England is a demonstration of the truth of our position. For where have the ultra views of Calvinism so generally prevailed, as in New England? And nowhere has Universalism and its kindred errors made such progress as here.

We have no doubt but they would have continued to have spread, until they would have covered the whole country occupied by the descendants of the "pilgrim fathers," but for the timely introduction of a purer doctrine — the leaven of *truth and consistency*, which is not only found among Methodists, but has been infused by them more or less into all the different evangelical churches of New England. It has accomplished a moral revolution, no less real, because it has not always been realized, and scarcely ever acknowledged, by those who have been thus signally benefited. Who does not know that the preaching of even Calvinist churches, however Calvinistic their creed, is entirely different from what it was thirty or fifty years ago? We write not these things in malice or unkindness; far from it. Great good has been accomplished by Calvinist churches, and they are doing a great work at the present day, in spreading the gospel through the world Among them are a host of noble, talented men, who are laboring sincerely, and in many cases successfully, for the conversion of the world to Christ. And we cheerfully bid them a *hearty* God speed, one and all; we have none of that spirit that would forbid any man or class of men from casting out devils, because he followeth not us. But as Methodists we believe that the good they accomplish is the fruit of the *great and fundamental truths* of the gospel which they hold, and advocate with a most commendable zeal; and rather in spite of their Calvinism than by means of it. And the fact, that in all cases of revival among them (so far as our knowledge extends) the peculiar doctrines of Calvinism are entirely laid aside for the time being, and a purer and simpler doctrine is preached, not unlike that taught by Methodists, is a strong evidence of the correctness of the opinion.

It may be proper to introduce here a brief statement of the doctrine of election, as held by the Methodist Church. It is often said that Methodists do not believe in election; but it is a mistake. They believe in what they consider Bible election, but not in Calvinistic election. They believe that God has foreordained and decreed, not "whatsoever comes to pass," but certain things, such as — that he would make man a moral agent, and in all things treat him as such; that he would provide a *full* and *free* salvation for *all men*, and offer it to all, without partiality; that he that believed and obeyed the gospel, should be saved, and he that believed not should be damned.

There are three kinds of election spoken of in the Bible, viz., persons elected or chosen to perform some particular work, or fill some particular office, as Cyrus was God's elect or God's chosen, to rebuild the temple; Paul was elected to preach the gospel to the Gentiles. A second kind of election spoken of, is the election of nations or classes of men to certain privileges, as the Jews, or the posterity of Jacob, were elected in preference to the posterity of Esau, to enjoy the peculiar privileges conferred on that people, such as receiving the Law, preserving the knowledge of the true God, and his word, and "of whom, as concerning the flesh, Christ came, who is God over all." This is a collective election, and does not necessarily affect the final salvation of the soul; for we are taught that many of these elect Jews perished on account of their sins. (See 1 Cor., chap. x.) Another instance of this kind of election is the calling or election of the Gentiles, in the time of Christ and his apostles, to the enjoyment of equal privileges with the Jews under the gospel. Of this election the apostle treats in his letter to the Romans, and to the Ephesians, as one may plainly see, by reading them with this fact before the mind; and it will afford a ready and satisfactory explanation to all those passages which have been considered the stronghold of Calvinism. Paul in his letter to Rome is writing to Jews who were greatly displeased with the idea that the Gentiles were to be put on an equality with them through the gospel, and especially that they were to be "broken off," and the Gentiles grafted in. Paul labors to show them that they were broken off or rejected because of their unbelief, and that the election of the Gentiles was not only reasonable and right, but that it was according to the foreordination and purpose of God, and in perfect keeping with God's dealings with *the Jews*, in calling or electing them in preference to the descendants of Esau. He treats not of individuals, but of nations. In the reference to Jacob and Esau, you will see, by noticing the context and the passage in Malachi from which the apostle quotes, that he is speaking of their posterity. He says, "It was said unto her, the elder shall serve the younger." Now it is not true that Esau ever did serve Jacob in person: but the posterity of Esau did serve the posterity of Jacob. In Malachi it is said, "And I hated Esau, and laid his mountains and his heritage waste for the dragons of the wilderness." This was not spoken or fulfilled concerning the heritage of Esau personally, but concerning his posterity, the Edomites. "Let it be remembered, 1. That there is not a word spoken here concerning the *eternal state* of either Jacob or Esau. 2. That what is spoken concerns merely their *earthly possessions*. And, 3. That it does not concern the *two brothers* at all, but the posterity of each." (See Dr. A. Clarke's comments on these passages and the subject generally.) Another, and the only kind of personal election to eternal life, found in the Bible, is the election through grace of all that believe and obey the gospel. Or as Peter has it, "elect according to the foreknowledge of God the Father, *through* sanctification of the spirit, unto obedience, and sprinkling of the blood of Jesus Christ." Mr. Wesley says, "Strictly speaking, there is no *foreknowledge*, no more than *afterknowledge*, with God; but all things are known to him as *present*, from eternity to eternity. *Election*, in the Scriptural sense, is God's doing any thing that our merit or power has no part in. The true predestination or fore appointment of God, is, 1. He that believeth shall be saved from the guilt and power of sin. 2. He that endureth to the end shall be saved eternally. 3. They who *receive* the precious gift of faith thereby become the sons of God; and being sons, they shall receive the spirit of holiness, to walk as Christ also walked. Throughout every part of this appointment of God, *promise* and *duty* go hand in hand. All is free gift; and yet, such is the gift, that it depends in the final issue on our future obedience to the heavenly call. But other predestination than this, either to life or death eternal, the Scripture knows not of: moreover, 1. It is a cruel respect of persons; an unjust regard of one, and an unjust disregard of another: it is mere *creature partiality*, and not *infinite justice*. 2. It is not *plain* Scripture doctrine, (if true,) but rather inconsistent with the express written word that speaks of God's universal offers of grace; his invitations, promises, threatenings, being all *general*. 3. We are bid to choose life, and reprehended for not doing it. 4. It is inconsistent with a state of probation in those that *must* be saved, or *must* be lost. 5. It is of fatal consequence."

CHAPTER III.

THE SACRAMENTS.

We shall next notice the sentiments of the Methodist Church in reference to the Sacraments—Baptism, and the Lord's Supper.

On the subject of baptism, Methodists are Pedo-Baptists. And although they do not make these views of the proper subjects or mode of baptism a test of communion or church membership, yet as a church they believe that baptism is both a sign and seal; an external and visible sign of an internal and invisible work of grace, accomplished in the heart by the Spirit purifying the soul. It is a *sign* of the righteousness we have through the covenant of grace. It is also a sign and seal of that covenant between God and our souls; a solemn and public acknowledgment on our part of this covenant relation, and consequently of its obligations. It is a public profession of our faith in Christ the only Saviour

That believers and their infant children are the proper subjects of baptism, they think is evident from the following considerations:

1. Baptism was manifestly considered by Christ and the apostles as succeeding the rite of circumcision, as the Lord's Supper is admitted to have succeeded that of the Passover. As the former rite was to be administered to believers and their children, so it would be expected that the one succeeding it would be extended to them, unless prohibited, and no such prohibition is to be found. If the infant children of believers were then entitled to the covenant benefits of circumcision, so they are now entitled to the covenant benefits of baptism. Here let it be remembered, that the covenant of which circumcision was the seal is in all essential points the same as that of which baptism is the seal. It is not, therefore, as some say, a rite of the old covenant, and consequently no longer in use; it is the rite or seal of the Abrahamic covenant of faith. Abraham received the sign of circumcision as "a seal of the righteousness he then had, which was a righteousness of faith." "Abraham believed God, and it was accounted to him

for righteousness." The church is therefore essentially the same now as then; only its principles have been more fully developed, perfected, and brought to light through the gospel, and in all things adapted to the present stage of the church under the fulness of the gospel dispensation. Consequently either one of the prominent rites of the church has been entirely lost, or the more reasonable conclusion follows, viz., that baptism takes the place of circumcision. Therefore as the original rite was extended to to the child, so (unless prohibited, which is not even pretended) should the substitute be. These words of Paul in his letter to the Colossians settle the relation between baptism and circumcision: "In whom also ye are circumcised with the circumcision made without hands, in putting off the body of the sins of the flesh, by the circumcision of Christ; buried with him in baptism." Does any one teach you to be circumcised? This is our circumcision, even baptism. This was the sentiment of the primitive church. Justin Martyr, who lived forty years after the apostles, says: "We, who by him (Christ) have had access to God, have not received this carnal circumcision, but spiritual, and we have received it by baptism." Again he says, "*We are circumcised by baptism, with Christ's circumcision.*"

2. Children are declared by Christ to be members of his kingdom. "Suffer the *little* children to come unto me and forbid them not; for of such is the kingdom of heaven." If they are included in the covenant of grace, as nearly all at the present day profess to believe, why deny them the rite and seal of that covenant?

3. The Saviour commanded his disciples to "go and teach (make proselytes of) all nations, baptizing them," &c. Now these disciples were familiar with the manner of making proselytes to the Jewish religion, and they would naturally understand that they were to go forth and make proselytes to Christ's religion in the same way, as they were directed to use the same ceremony, unless told to the contrary, of which there is no intimation; and the Jews' custom was to receive parents and their children by baptism as proselytes. They would naturally, therefore, pursue the same course with those who became proselytes to the Christian religion.

4. It is said in the Scriptures that the apostles baptized the households of them that believed. The cases of Lydia and the jailer are instances. These facts are recorded in a way which would naturally lead the reader to believe that children were baptized. This, though not absolutely certain, is yet highly probable, as families are generally made up in part of children. Peter's language on the day of Pentecost has the same tendency. Addressing himself to the Jews, who had always considered their children as included in the covenant privileges, he says, "For the promise is to you, and *your children*," &c. Who can believe that the Jews would have given up, without the least controversy or objection, a privilege and ordinance for which they had ever had the most sacred and affectionate regard? Yet no controversy existed between the believing Jews and the primitive church on this subject. I see a company of Jewish parents, who have embraced Christianity, and in accordance with their custom and duty in all past ages of the church, they come to present their children before God, but the disciples, for some cause, object. They appeal to the Master. Now an

important question is to be settled, one of infinite interest to every Jew, viz., whether their children are to be recognized, in the initiatory ordinance of the *Christian* church, or not? The Saviour replies, "Suffer little children to come unto me, and forbid them not, for of such is the kingdom of Heaven." The question is settled, and the Jew is satisfied; their children are recognized. No controversy existed on the subject for eleven hundred years.

5. That the whole primitive church practiced infant baptism, is evident from the following quotations from the early fathers. Justin Martyr, who lived forty years after the apostles, speaking of members of the church, says, "a part of these were sixty or seventy years of age, who were made disciples of Christ from their *infancy*." Consequently they must have been so made (that is baptized) in the time of the apostles. Thus the practice of infant baptism in the age of the apostles, is proved by one of the earliest and most credible Christian writers. Ireneus, who was a disciple of Polycarp, who was himself a disciple of St. John, says, "Christ came to save all persons who by

him are baptized under God; infants and little ones, children, youth and elder persons." Origen, who was born in the second century, says, "The church hath received the tradition *from the apostles*, that baptism ought to be administered to infants." Tertullian also bears his testimony to the practice of infant baptism. Cyprian, who was also born in the second century, says that "sixty-six bishops being convened at Carthage, having the question referred to them, whether infants might be baptized before they were eight days old, decided unanimously that no infant is to be prohibited the benefit of baptism." Gregory Nazianzen, of the fourth century, says, "The whole church practices infant baptism; it was not instituted by councils, but was always in use." Pellagias declared that he had "never heard even an impious heretic who asserted that infants are not to be baptized." Ambrose and Augustine, the great luminaries of the age, bear their positive testimony to the practice of infant baptism from the first. Augustine says, "It came not by any council, or by any authority *later* or *less* than that of the apostles."

The antiquity of infant baptism, as proved by

these quotations from the early fathers, furnishes evidence of its divine authority that cannot be successfully controverted. If the infant children of believers were not baptized in the days of the apostles, when did the practice commence? If introduced after the apostolic age, it must have been a great innovation. But no mention is made by any writer of its introduction, nor of any controversy, which must necessarily have grown out of such an innovation; nor does it appear that any one ever questioned its propriety or validity until the twelfth century, when it was started by Peter Bruis, a Frenchman, whose followers were called Peter Brusians. And then in the fifteenth century, by the Ana-Baptists, in Germany. Only about two hundred years after Christ we see sixty-six pastors convened in a council, having the subject of infant baptism distinctly before them, and not one even intimates that he has a doubt of the validity of the practice, but, on the contrary, they unanimously resolve that no infant, however young, shall be prohibited from this rite. Certainly, if the apostles and their converts were all Baptists, as we are told, they had lost ground strangely to have become extinct in so short a time; and they must have been a different kind of Baptists from those of the present day, to have given up without controversy. But we cannot believe this to have been the case, but must believe with Origen, that the church received this practice from the apostles.

6. We close the argument by presenting the statements of two individuals, whose testimony ought to have an influence with every Christian. "Mr. Wolff, the celebrated converted Jew, and missionary among that people, informs us, that in his wanderings in the interior of Asia he found, in a retired spot, a small village of Christians surrounded by Mohammedans. They have remained there from time immemorial, undisturbed amid the changes which have been going on around them in the distant parts of the earth. Mr. Wolff, among other questions which he put to them, asked them if they baptized their children; they answered, "Yes, always." "How do you do it?" "We take them to the water, hold them over it, and sprinkle water upon them in the name of the Father and the Son and the

Holy Ghost." And they aver this to have been their practice from the time of John the Baptist. The other witness is the Nestorian Bishop, Mar Yohanan, who came to this country in company with Mr. Perkins from the interior of Asia. The church over which he was set had preserved their primitive simplicity, and the form of church government which had universally prevailed in the times immediately following the days of the apostles; they had no connection with the Roman or Greek churches. In a conversation with some gentlemen in New York, Mar Yohanan was asked, "Do you baptize infants?" "Yes, always; every child is baptized." "How do you baptize adults?" "We have none to baptize; every child as soon as possible is baptized." No modern Baptist can say that with them this practice is of Popish origin, inasmuch as they have had no connection with that hierarchy. When asked, "How do you regard the Roman and Greek churches?" Mar Yohanan replied, "We love them not; no good; we from the apostles; we pray not to the Virgin Mary; we have no relics, no images, in our churches; one simple wooden cross, that's all." These recently developed facts, are strong evidences of both the antiquity and validity of infant baptism.

7. But we are asked, and it is a very common objection, "What good will it do infants to baptize them?" Abraham might have inquired of Jehovah, by way of objection, "What good will it do to circumcise my children?" with equal if not greater propriety. What do you think would have been the result? But his faith was so strong in the Lord that he did not stop to question the utility of obedience for a moment. We would suggest to such inquirers the propriety of imitating the faith of Abraham. But we might ask in return, what good does it do any one to be baptized? Does the mere act of applying water to the person, though they be entirely covered with it, do them any good? But it is our duty! Very well, so we believe this to be. Thus this objection is equally valid in one case as in the other. But you say you do not believe it is a duty to baptize infants; and so the Friend Quaker says of all baptisms by water.

But it does the parents good. They feel that "the vows of God are upon them." They will feel more sensibly their obligation to train up their children for God, having consecrated them to him in this public and solemn manner. It will do the child good, if the parents are faithful in admonishing and instructing him in regard to it. It will hold a restraining influence over him in after life; he will not forget it; it will give interest and weight to the obligation urged upon him to early dedicate himself to God. Says Matthew Henry, the learned and pious commentator upon the bible, "I cannot but take occasion to express my gratitude to God for my infant baptism; not only as it was an early admission into the visible body of Christ, but as it furnished my parents with a good argument, and I trust through grace a prevailing argument, for an early dedication of myself to God. If God has wrought any good work upon my soul, I desire with humble thankfulness to acknowledge the influence of my *infant baptism* upon it."

8. But it is said, "If we have our children baptized, they may be dissatisfied with it when they come to years of understanding." This would never be the case, we confidently believe, if parents would do their duty. If they would

take half the pains to instruct their children in the nature and validity of their baptism, that Baptists do to make them dissatisfied with it, there would be few if any who would be in the least dissatisfied with their baptism. The trouble is, we leave the mind wholly uninformed on this subject, and the Baptists are diligent in storing it with their objections and peculiar sentiments. Let us but do our duty, and God will take care of the result. "But the Bible says, *Believe* and be baptized." So the Bible says, "he that believeth not, shall be damned." Now if the former excludes infants from baptism, the latter excludes them from heaven. But Baptists are shocked at the thought of this, and some even deny (what every one may know to be true) that they ever believed in the damnation of a portion of those dying in infancy. Though few if any at the present day believe this, Methodism has made them ashamed of it, in teaching a better way.

But it is objected finally, "There is no positive precept or Bible for infant baptism." No more is there for female communion, or the observance of the first day of the week for the

Sabbath; and it is contended that the latter rests on precisely the same kind of testimony as the practice of infant baptism, viz., an original institution; the practice of the apostles, as inferred from the Scriptures; and the sanction of the whole primitive church. Hence it appears that the only consistent Baptists are those who reject the first-day Sabbath, and keep the seventh, called Seventh-day Baptists.

But, as we remarked at the commencement of this subject, though as a body Methodists believe in infant baptism, yet as they do not purpose to exclude any true Christians from the church, and considering the present excited state of this controversy on the side of the opposers of infant baptism, it is to be expected that many will be undecided in regard to their duty, while others will be strongly prejudiced against infant baptism, they do not *require* their members to practice infant baptism. They place the subject in what they regard as the true light before them, and leave them to act according to their convictions of duty, to answer their own consciences before God, as in other matters not essential to salvation.

CHAPTER IV.

THE MODE OF BAPTISM.

As Methodists believe that baptism is an outward visible sign of an inward and invisible work of grace, as well as a covenant seal of our consecration to God, so they believe that the application of water (without regard to quantity) to a proper candidate, by a proper administrator, in the name of the Trinity, is valid baptism. They give, therefore, to every person desiring the ordinance at their hands, the choice as to the mode. If immersion is desired, they immerse; if sprinkling is preferred, or pouring, they regard it equally valid and no less acceptable to God.

It is not, therefore, necessary for Methodists or any Pedo-Baptist to disprove the practice or validity of immersion, nor have they any desire to do it, but simply to disprove exclusive immersion, or the sentiment of the Baptists that immersion is the only mode of baptism. The labor therefore is all on their side, and it only remains for us to refute their arguments.

They confidently assert that the literal and only meaning of the word baptize, is to immerse; and that the translators of the Scriptures are verily guilty for not having so translated the original "baptizo," to which, they say, they only gave an English ending, to please the king, or somebody else. Hence their Baptist Bible was prepared, a few years since, to finish what the translators left imperfect; but it proved a splendid failure. What are the facts in reference to the translation of this word? Simply these; the translators found in the Scriptures a number of words in the original, each one of which were used in a variety of different senses; and also others, the meaning of which could not be expressed by any one English word. This every Greek scholar knows to be the case in that language. Among these words was "baptizo," which, though it might admit of the term immersion in English, in many instances, yet in others it was altogether improper, and inconsistent both with the Scriptures and matter of fact. Take the following as examples. "I indeed (immerse) you with water, &c., but there cometh one, who shall (immerse) you with the Holy Ghost and with fire." What an idea! Again, notice the Saviour's promise: "For John indeed (immersed) with water, but ye shall be (immersed) with the Holy Ghost not many days hence." Now, besides this being monstrously absurd in itself, it does not agree with the manner of the fulfilment of the promise, for it is said, "And they were all *filled* with the Holy Ghost," not immersed with it. The apostle, speaking of the children of Israel, says, "they were all baptized unto Moses in the cloud and in the sea." To say they were immersed unto Moses would be to testify falsely, as the Bible says they went through "*dry shod*." But says the Baptist, "They were surrounded with water, and were therefore immersed." But he should remember that the Holy Ghost saith that the "pillar of cloud" was behind them at this time, to screen them from their enemies; and as there was no water above, beneath, or before them, and the Scriptures assert that they went through "dry shod," they could not in any proper sense be said to be immersed. It is very easy to prove that the Egyptians were immersed, but not the children of Israel. These were some of the many difficulties which presented themselves to the minds of the translators, in regard to this and other words of the same character. Hence they agreed to leave all such words untranslated, merely giving them an English form; and who does not see the wisdom of such a course? It is much easier to find fault with a piece of work, than it is to improve it. So we conclude our Baptist brethren found it, as they seem themselves little pleased with their new Baptist Bible. It may do to give such to the poor heathen who have seen no other, but it will never succeed among enlightened, Christian people. That the word baptizo means to immerse, we admit, but that it never means any thing else we deny. We read in one of the classical writers, of "baptizing the sea with the blood of a mouse." Now we do not think that even the Baptists' faith would be strong enough here, to enable him to believe that the sea was immersed in the blood of the mouse. The meaning is plain, the sea was sprinkled with the blood, but the Greek writer uses the term baptizo. Numerous are the instances where the word is used by the best Greek writers with the above meaning, and also to pour, to wash, to purify, cleanse, &c. Greek lexicons give to this word the following meanings, "to dip, immerse, to wash, cleanse, purify, sprinkle," &c. Bapto, from which it is derived, has the following meanings: "to dip, plunge, immerse, wash, to wet, moisten, sprinkle, to steep, imbue, to dye, stain, color."

It is very common for words to so change their signification, as to come to signify that for which the thing originally signified was used. Thus bapto originally signified to dip, but as things were generally dyed by dipping, it came in process of time to signify to dye, to stain, &c. So with the word baptizo, its derivative; as things were dipped, plunged, washed, &c., to cleanse, or to purify, it was used in this sense as we have seen. The ground we advocate, is, that baptizo, when used in a ritual sense in the New Testament, signifies to purify or cleanse, without any reference to the mode of purification, save it be by water, as an emblem.

We believe this for the following reasons: 1. Nothing less than this would have been sufficiently definite and significant. The title or command should give some definite idea as tc the nature or design of the rite enjoined. But suppose the Saviour to have commanded his disciples to go teach, and immerse, that is, place the disciples under water, what signification would the command have had? What clue to the thing signified would have been given by this? Persons are put into the water for various purposes. But suppose we understand the Saviour as saying "Go teach (make disciples of) all nations, purifying them," &c. This would make the design evident; baptizo, the title, would then signify the grand object of the rite, the intention of the ceremonial use of water, namely, to represent the purification of the heart by the Holy Ghost.

2. The Jews expected that the Messiah would purify, when he came, for this had been foretold of him; but nowhere was it said he should immerse. Malachi said, "He shall purify the sons of Levi," &c. John reiterates it, saying, "He shall baptize you with the Holy Ghost and

with fire," using the term baptizo in the sense of to purify. The inquiry of the Jews, "Why baptizest thou, if thou art not the Christ?" shows that they used it in this sense. It had been foretold of the Messiah that he should purify; they understood all this literally; and when a great purifier appears, as John the Baptist, they at once go out to see him; and he says "I am not the Christ." They inquire at once, "Why baptizest (purifiest) thou then, if thou art not the Christ?"

3. The contrast made by John between his baptism and that of Christ, sustains and illustrates this view of baptizo. He says, "I indeed baptize you with water, but he shall baptize you with the Holy Ghost and fire." Now whatever baptize means in one sentence, it means in the other. Hence if we say it means immerse, then we read, I indeed immerse you with water, but he shall immerse or dip you with the Holy Ghost and fire. How unmeaning! How much more natural and intelligent to read, I indeed purify or cleanse you with water, but he shall purify you with the Holy Ghost and fire.

4. The analogy between water and spiritua baptism is another proof of this view. We have seen that John represents them as closely connected. The Scriptures speak of the Spirit's "purifying us," "cleansing our hearts," of its being "poured upon us," our hearts are said to be "filled" with it, "sprinkled from an evil conscience," &c., but never of immersing us in the Spirit, or dipping us in the Holy Ghost and fire. Yet this must be the reading of many passages if baptizo invariably means to immerse or dip.

5. The Scriptures also sustain this signification: Mark vii. 4; "And when they came from the market, except they baptizontai (in English, wash or purify,) they eat not." Luke xi. 38; "And when the Pharisee saw it, he marvelled that he had not ebaptisthe (in English, washed or been purified) before dinner." Their manner of washing was for the servant to pour water on their hands. They also baptizontai, purified or washed their tables, beds, or couches, &c. That they did not immerse themselves before every meal is evident. Still more so that they did not immerse their tables, couches,

&c., but they purified them with water. The Saviour's reply to the Pharisee shows that he understood the term in the sense of purify. The Pharisee marvelled that he had not ebap tisthe before dinner. The Saviour replied, "Now do ye Pharisees katharizete, make clean, or purify the outside," &c., interpreting baptizo with katharizo, which invariably means to purify. John iii. 25, 26; "Then there arose a question between some of John's disciples and the Jews about (katharismon,) purifying. And they came to John and said, Rabbi, he that was with us beyond Jordan, to whom thou bearest witness, the same baptizeth, and all men come to him." Here is the clearest possible evidence that baptizo is used in the New Testament, in the sense of katharizo, to purify. A question arose about purifying, and to settle it, they come to John and present the question, but use the term baptizo, or baptizeth. This shows that they used the two words, baptizo and katharizo in the same sense, that is, to purify. With this signification the command to baptize, in all its varied connections, will be found plain and intelligible, while with the sense of immerse, it is not only unmeaning but often contradictory. But it is said the apostles immersed, and their example is sufficient. This may have been the case, but there is no positive proof of it. There is not an instance mentioned in the Bible but which admits of a reasonable explanation without involving the practice of immersion. Philip and the Eunuch went down into the water, but that does not prove that Philip immersed him. Besides, there are many difficulties in the way of such interpretation; such as changing raiment under those circumstances, by a man on a journey, and receiving the ordinance by the side of the highway; besides, no intimation is given of such preparation. The scarcity of water in that country sufficient to immerse, presents another obstacle. The Saviour went *into* the mountain, but we do not suppose he went under the mountain. It is a well known fact that the prepositions *into* and *out of* may, and often do signify merely *to* and *from*, and might have been so translated with perfect propriety. But if it be admitted that the apostles did baptize by immersion, in this and many other instances where it is contended for, yet it proves nothing for exclusive immersion. There are many other instances recorded where it is at least *as* evident that they were not immersed: the day of Pentecost, when three thousand were baptized; the jailer and his house, baptized by a prisoner at the dead of night; and even the case of John, of whom it is said, "And there went out to him all Jerusalem and *all* Judea, and all the region round about Jordan, and were baptized of him." Can any one suppose that he immersed this multitude during his short ministry? Some writers suppose as many as two million were baptized by him; and some Baptist writers have supposed that as many as *five hundred thousand* were *immersed*. Now his ministry continued one year and a half. Allowing one minute for each person, to baptize that number he must have stood in the water sixteen hours per day for the entire time of his ministry! But it is said, "*John did no miracle.*" Certainly then he could not have done this, or baptized this number by immersion.

The children of Israel though not baptized by the apostles, yet Paul the apostle says they were baptized; and yet, as we have seen, they could not as a matter of fact have been immersed, neither in the "sea" nor in the "cloud." Nothing, therefore, can be determined by the example of the apostles in this matter. But it is said the early Christian church practiced immersion. They also baptized the candidate in a state of nudity, but they did not even pretend that immersion was essential to the validity of the ordinance, but merely as preferable to other modes which they regarded as valid.

But there is no positive proof of the practice of sprinkling in the Bible, says the Baptist. Where is your thus saith the Lord? Can you put your finger on the passage that proves it? they confidently exclaim. To all this we reply, where is your thus saith the Lord for immersion? Can *you* put *your finger* on the passage that proves it? No! For it is not in the Bible, not even the word immerse. But baptizo means to immerse and nothing else. That is not only denied, but we have already proved it false by the Bible itself. Well, says the Baptist, it is plain enough! But that is only your inference, not a positive precept. Others think it is plain enough that sprinkling is baptism, and that it was practiced in the apostles' times.

There is another argument much used by Baptists, and one by means of which they have induced more young converts to be immersed than by all others, viz., "Christ was immersed, and we ought to follow his example, for he was baptized as an example for us." Now the first premise is assumed. That Christ *was* immersed cannot be proved. He came up *out of* the water, but that does not prove his immersion; besides, as we have noticed, the preposition which is translated "out of" has a variety of meanings, and might be rendered *from* with equal propriety. So if the translators (with whom the Baptists find so much fault for not doing their work better) had translated it thus, He went up straightway *from* the water, then there would have been no *appearance* of immersion. But there is not the least evidence that he was baptized as an example for us. And the fact that he could not be baptized in the name of the Trinity, which is essential to Christian baptism, that he could not be baptized upon a profession of his faith in himself, nor for washing away his sins, emblematically, nor unto repentance to prepare the way for his own coming, according to the practice and design of John's baptism, is conclusive evidence that his baptism was essentially different from all other Christian baptisms, and could not have been intended as an example for us. But if the mode of his baptism be an example for us to follow, then the *time* of his baptism is also an example for us. But he was not baptized till about thirty years of age; therefore, if we must follow his example, we must wait till we arrive at the same age or have been pious as long. But who believes that? Methinks I hear the Baptist say, "Why tarriest thou? arise and be baptized."

Again, if he was baptized as an example for us, why did he not partake of the sacrament of the supper for the same end? But this he did not do. Nor is there the least possible evidence that he is our example in baptism. He was baptized "to fulfil all righteousness." The Law required that every priest should be washed or baptized with water, and in obedience to that law, he being about to fulfil the great work of the priest in making atonement for the sins of the people, submitted to that ordinance of the law. But it is said, "He was not in the regular line of the priesthood." But this no more released or excluded him from the ceremonies of that office, than it excluded him from the office, or prevented his making atonement for sin as our high priest.

Another favorite argument with the Baptists is this: "Baptism is designed to represent the death, burial, and resurrection of Christ; and this can only be done by our being buried in, and raised up out of the water." But the Scriptures nowhere represent this to be the design of baptism. And how, we ask, does immersion represent the death of Christ? He died on the cross, suspended between the heavens and the earth, and who ever heard of a person being immersed in that manner? This would be quite as bad as sprinkling, which causes such horror to the Baptists. The candidate's being raised out of the water represents his coming forth from the tomb about as truly. There are passages of Scripture on which this opinion is founded which we will examine. Rom. vi. 2, &c. "How shall we that are *dead* to sin live any longer therein: know ye not that so many of us as were (are) baptized into Jesus Christ (into or to faith in Christ) were *baptized* into (or to a faith in) his death? therefore we are buried with him by baptism into his death, that like as Christ was raised up from the dead by the glory of the Father, even so also we should walk in newness of life." Now here is no reference to the mode of baptism at all, but the idea is simply this: As Christ died for sin, (and buried simply denotes death,) so we should reckon ourselves dead with him, unto sin, and baptism is a sign of that death or separation from sin. Now unless Christ had been put to death by being *buried alive*, there can be traced no resemblance between immersion and his death. Much is said of "Christ's *liquid grave*," but we have never seen it, or found it in the Bible. Men ought to *blush*, and would, but for the hardening influences of bigotry and fanaticism, to be heard exhorting converts to follow "their Saviour down into *his liquid grave*." But the apostle uses two other metaphors here to express the connection of a redeemed sinner with the Saviour; "for if we have been planted together in the likeness of his *death,* (if we are dead to sin, as he was *for* sin,) we shall be also in the likeness of his resurrection;" that is, we shall be raised from a death of sin to a life of *holiness.*

Again: "Knowing this, that our old man (carnal nature) is crucified with him, — that henceforth we should not serve sin." The passage in Col. ii. 12, is of similar import, and admits of the same explanation.

The practice of immersion in cold climates, and especially at the cold season of the year, is altogether inconsistent with the mild and merciful economy of the gospel. Go to Greenland, and in the midst of the almost everlasting ice, with the streams frozen to the bottom, and their huts encased in ice formed from the breath of the inmates, and there proclaim to the people, "Believe and be immersed," and you would truly bind a "yoke upon them which neither we nor our fathers were able to bear," a duty which they could not possibly perform. "Only have faith and there is no danger," says the Baptist. We answer that it is not faith that is wanting, but caloric, or heat.

It is not only inconsistent with the economy of grace, but it renders obedience in many instances actually impossible. It is frequently the case that persons who have neglected religion in health, or having sought the Lord have for some reason neglected baptism, when they are brought to the gate of death wish to confess the Saviour and receive the sacrament before they die. But they cannot be immersed; sickness renders it absolutely impossible; must they be denied this privilege? To tell them that baptism is not their duty, would be to contradict the Bible. We could no more refuse the sacrament to such, and let them die in grief, than we could break the Sabbath, or profane God's holy name. If the Baptists can, they are welcome to their consciences and their faith. But these difficulties are often too much even for them. A little boy of a neighboring State, the son of a Baptist mother, became a happy Christian. He bore the pains of a lingering sickness with the utmost patience, rejoicing in the hope of a glorious immortality. A little before his death he desired to be baptized and receive the sacrament. Said the mother, You are so sick you cannot be taken up to be baptized. I know it, mother, said he, but I can be baptized in my cradle. Could the mother refuse? The Methodist minister was sent for, but being unordained, he called to his aid an Episcopalian, and repaired to the place, and little Robert was baptized. Arrangements were now made for the communion. The agitation of the anxious mother and her Baptist friends may easily be imagined. What could they do? Thank God, prejudice and sectarian proscription gave way, and they all knelt around the cradle, Episcopalians, Methodists, and Baptists, and with the dying saint solemnized the holy sacrament. Was this wrong? Let those believe it who can! We cannot.

It was in view of the foregoing reasons, scriptures, and facts, that my mind, after a long and hard struggle between these and previous opinions, yielded to the force of conviction, and I wholly renounced the doctrine of exclusive immersion.

CHAPTER V.

OPEN COMMUNION.

METHODISTS regard the sacrament of the Lord's Supper as an ordinance appointed by the Lord, to be repeated in the church till his coming again at the last day. "Do this in remembrance of me," "till I come." It is a commemoration of the sufferings and death of Christ; but it is more than a mere commemoration, for God has taught us to expect his special presence and blessing in the observance of this institution, and that faith is necessary in order to a proper observance of the same, for we must "discern the Lord's body," which we can do only through faith. Every person coming to the table of the Lord should expect to meet the Saviour and receive spiritual profit; to go away a better Christian than when he came, more heavenly minded, more like Christ. In order to be prepared to approach the table of the Lord, a person must be a practical believer in the doctrine of the vicarious atonement by Christ; in "Christ our sacrifice for sin," and the doctrine of justification by faith in Christ Jesus. By receiving the sacrament he says to the world that he believes these Gospel truths, and rests his hope of heaven on this foundation, and this alone. Every person possessing this qualification, and giving evidence of the same, has a right to come to the Lord's table. So Methodists believe and so they practice. It is the Lord's table, let none of his children be forbidden to approach it. They do not therefore regard baptism as an indispensable prerequisite to the communion. Though a desirable order, yet it is not an indispensable one. In accordance with these principles, they invite to the table of the Lord with them all persons in regular standing in any of the evangelical churches. But it is sometimes asked, why not invite all Christians, and say nothing about church membership? We answer: When a person is a member of a Christian church he is supposed to be a Christian; the church vouches for his Christian character, by receiving and retaining him within its pale; and on this their recommendation, or testimony, we welcome him to the communion, though he be a stranger to us. But to invite persons for whom no one is responsible, and of whom we know nothing, save that he says he is a Christian, would be to expose ourselves to imposition from those who claim to be Christians, though they give no evidence of it to others. There are not a few of this class at the present day. Hence the impropriety of a more general invitation. But those who are personally known as Christians are made welcome. There are persons who have experienced religion, but have not as yet been able to satisfy their minds in regard to the subject of baptism, (no strange occurrence in the midst of the conflicting sentiments of Baptists and others, and having no divinely inspired men as in the days of the apostles, to determine infallibly for us,) and wishing to act understandingly in all things, they have as yet deferred being baptized, or uniting with the church. Or they may have delayed it from some peculiarity in their circumstances, or for want of a convenient opportunity to be baptized, yet giving evidence to all that they are true disciples of Christ; such persons are welcome to the table of the Lord among Methodists. That this is the sentiment of the Methodist church as a body, (though some individuals may hold differently,) is evident not only from her practice and the writings of some of her most prominent men, but from the recent unanimous decision of the Bishops or Superintendents, viz.: "That baptism is not a Scriptural, and therefore not an indispensable, prerequisite to the communion." This, coming from the highest authority in the church, and approved by all, or at least nearly all of the ministry and membership, shows that it is the doctrine of the church.

And in perfect accordance with this is the language of the Discipline, as seen in its ritual. "Ye that do truly and earnestly repent of your sins, and are in love and charity with your neighbors, and intend to lead a new life, following the commandments of God, and walking henceforth in his holy ways, draw near with faith, and take this holy sacrament to your comfort; and make your humble confession to Almighty God, meekly kneeling upon your knees."

It may be proper here to take a little notice of a tract written by Rev. S. Remington, a Baptist minister, (formerly a Methodist clergyman,) and circulated quite extensively by the Baptist church, styled a "Defence of restricted communion," in which there are several things deserving of attention; not on account of the ability or candor manifested by the writer, but for the misrepresentations it contains, and the fact that they are endorsed and circulated by the Baptist church.

The author first assumes what is wholly void of truth, viz.: That Congregationalists, Methodists, and all others, agree perfectly with the Baptists, that baptism is an indispensable prerequisite to the communion; and then on this false assumption as a foundation, he proceeds to erect his building, the materials of which are of the same character. He says, "We agree that it (baptism) is one of the essential requisites of an admission to the Lord's table, and that none, however pious, ought to be permitted to enjoy this holy ordinance previous to a compliance with this Christian rite." This he thinks so "obvious" as to need no proof. He even intimates that it has never been "affirmed to the contrary," which it seems that he must have known to be untrue, especially as in the same woik, page 27, he mentions, by way of reproach, that a certain prominent Methodist minister had approved the contrary. And we have shown that not only one prominent man, but the church as a body, hold and practice the opposite. But he has condescended to attempt to furnish some proof of his position. His reference to the practice of the apostles will be answered in another place. He then quotes a number of authors, but not a Methodist writer is found in the whole list. Suppose we should affirm that all denominations agree that infants should be baptized, and quote a long list of Presbyterian and Congregationalist writers in proof; then assume the point as settled? What would the Baptists say to such proof? Yet we might do it with equal propriety! Still this false assumption is reiterated so frequently, that one is reminded of the saying that men generally in defending a weak point, make up what is wanting in argument by confident and unqualified assertions. But we are told, on page 36, that "The

Methodist E. Church, by a fair construction of her discipline, is far from being open in her communion." Now there is not a word in the Discipline to justify such a statement. The only argument which has the semblance of plausibility in it, is a quotation from a previous edition of our Discipline which was as follows. "Let no person that is not a member of our church be admitted to the communion without examination, and some token given by an elder or deacon. No person shall be admitted to the Lord's Supper among us, who is guilty of any practice for which we would exclude a member of our church."

Now this rule was adopted when some of the other denominations, with which we were associated in many places, did not make practical piety a condition of church membership; but Methodists, believing then as now that no impenitent or ungodly person should come to the communion, it was necessary to adopt some rule by which such persons, though they might belong to the church, could be prevented from coming to our communion. But the circumstances having so changed in this respect as to render this rule no longer necessary, or of any practical use, it remained on the statute book of the church as a dead letter until the last General Conference, when it was stricken out. Let the reader of this work of our Baptist friend keep this fact in mind. This quotation forms an essential part of every succeeding argument against Methodism, and yet in every instance is this and every other quotation from the Discipline, most manifestly, and it would seem wilfully perverted from the design and use of the same — as when he quotes the rule in reference to giving tickets for love-feasts, &c., an institution peculiar to Methodism, and applies it to the communion, to which he knew it had no reference whatever. He next quotes from the Discipline where it is stated that ministers and members who hold and disseminate doctrines contrary to those of our church, endeavoring to sow dissension in our societies, &c., shall be treated as in cases of gross immorality, or be expelled. He then attempts to prove that because we expel those ministers and members who, having in the most solemn manner professed their faith in the doctrines of the church, and promised to observe its usages, violate all their obligations, and acting the part of traitors, makes use of their hypocritical profession, or connection with the church, in order to injure it, that, therefore, we have no right to commune with those ministers and members of other churches (differing in some points of doctrine from us) who have always acted in perfect consistency with their profession. Wonderful logic this! Here we find the erased rule dragged in to meet a case entirely remote from that for which it was designed.

Another instance of perversion is found on page 41, where, to make out his point against the Methodists, he professes to quote the rule relating to members set aside for a breach of our rules; but quotes the one referring to those expelled from the church for immorality. Now we cannot suppose him so ignorant as not to know that this was an utter perversion of the Discipline, which contains two distinct rules for the trial of these different classes of persons. But he entirely disregards this distinction, and applies what is said of persons expelled for immorality to those set aside for breach of rules.

On the next page we find him repeating this manifest and strange perversion of the Discipline, and adding again the expunged rule, and professing with the help of these, to prove that because the Methodist Church requires her members to attend class-meetings, she has no right to commune with members of other denominations, who do not regularly attend class, though no such institution exists among them! Yes, he says: "Their rule says that they shall not be admitted." Now we do not like to say that he *knew* that was false; but we are constrained to exclaim, Poor human nature, how strangely will prejudice and bigotry blind thine eyes! The man who resorts to such reasoning to sustain his position, must have a bad *cause* to support, to say the least; but this is the sum of his arguments to prove that Methodists do not hold to open communion. Yet he has the audacity to affirm, in opposition to reason and facts, that "The Methodist Episcopal Church is close communion." He is also very liberal in dealing out his charges of inconsistency, "violation of conscience," &c. Now all this will pass for sense and logic with bigoted sectarians; but all other minds will form a very different opinion. It is a strong argument in favor of Methodism, that a man who seems determined, even at the sacrifice of logic and sense, to find something against it, can find nothing more reasonable than these manifest perversions and misrepresentations. But the writer informs his readers in his preface, with an air of self-consequence, that he has been "stationed in eight different cities," and therefore must know all about Methodism; as though his having been stationed in that number of cities was an important fact to prove his knowledge of Methodism! We know that some restless spirits do manage to go (or be sent) from city to city, stopping only a year perhaps in a place; but we are not aware that such persons have any more correct knowledge of Methodism than others; and such a reputation is by no means enviable. The ability and standing of *Methodist ministers* is not to be determined by the fact of their having been stationed in one or a dozen cities, or over wealthy churches. They are stationed according to the wants of the people, not according to their fulness.

As the question, Is baptism an indispensable prerequisite to the communion? is an important one; for the only hope of the Baptists is in sustaining this point; therefore in order to lay the subject fully before the reader, with the arguments for and against, and at the same time answering the Scripture argument of Mr. Remington, we here present an extract from a "Review of Rev. Jacob Knapp's sermon on restricted and mixed communion, by Rev. J. Porter." The circumstances, it appears, were these: Elder Knapp, a celebrated Baptist revivalist, visited Boston, and in perfect accordance with the practice of his colleagues, Andrews and others, represented himself, and was represented by his friends, as the decided antagonist of narrow sectarianism, and immediately began to denounce the "sectarian devil" as the powerful enemy (to the progress) of pure Christianity; and threatened to drive him from the city. By such professions he secured the co-operation of most of the Evangelical churches to aid and sustain him and his meetings. The result was, that a large number professed conversion. But when about to leave, Mr. Knapp had the notice circulated, that he would preach at such a time his farewell sermon to the young converts. The plot thus artfully laid, he, in accordance with his exclusive sentiments, and as Baptists are wont to do, improved, by preaching a sermon in favor of restricted, and against open or mixed communion.

His Baptist friends regarding it as a triumph, caught at once the zeal of their leader, and had the sermon published, and distributed it gratuitously among the young converts. This, others thought, looked a little like inviting "his Majesty," the "Sectarian Devil," back, but perhaps it was merely uncovering his "foot," which had been concealed for a time as a matter of policy. Elder Knapp being one of their strong men, and not a man who deals in weak arguments, where better are to be obtained, we may properly regard his arguments in favor of baptism as a necessary prerequisite to the communion, the strongest, if not the only ones, to be found. "Mr. K. takes the position 'that no person, however pious, has a right to participate at the Lord's Supper until baptized.' In proof of this he refers to the apostolic example as indubitable evidence, and exhibits that example in several Scriptures, of which the following is a specimen: 'Then Peter said unto them, repent and be baptized, every one of you. Then they that gladly received his word were baptized, and the same day there were added unto them about 3000 souls.' Not to question here what is intended to be proved by these Scriptures, viz.: that the practice of the apostles was, first to baptize their converts and then administer the sacrament, I remark, to constitute their examples into a valid and sufficient argument, it must be shown,

"1. That it has the force of a divine precept. 2. That they regarded baptism an indispensable *prerequisite* to the communion, so that the communion could not be administered properly without it. And 3. That circumstances in the constitution of the church have not so altered, that some persons may properly receive the communion who have not been baptized.

"The right or wrong of partaking of the communion before baptism, depends entirely on the will of God. Now the question is, was the example of the apostles in the premises designed as an expression of the will of God concerning us? Mr. K. assumes the affirmative; we deny it, and call for proof. If God designed by these historical references to teach us the duty of receiving and administering baptism before we do the communion, he designed that we should be baptized and join the church the same day we believe, and do every thing else in the way the apostles did. For if apostolic history has the authority of law in one particular, where it is not attended by express precept, it has the same authority in every other particular. Hence we are under the same obligation to have all things common, to have the sacrament in the night, and in an upper room, that we are to be baptized before partaking of it. Admitting for argument's sake, that the example attributed to the apostles, has the authority of law, the next point for Mr. K. to prove is, that they administered baptism as a *prerequisite* to the communion, so that without receiving the first the latter could not be properly administered. This is the main point in the discussion — the hinge upon which the whole turns. But where is the proof? Not the least particle is offered, neither can it be produced. Hence, says (the Baptist) Mr. (Robert) Hall, 'We affirm that in no part of the Scripture is it (baptism) inculcated as a *preparative to the Lord's Supper*, and that this view of it is a mere fiction of the imagination!' But had he proved this point, he must have shown one thing more before apostolic example would have met the necessities of his case, viz.: that the circumstances of the church have not so altered that some may properly receive the sacrament who have not been baptized. This he has not attempted. The apostles were inspired. They knew the will of God and had power to demonstrate their knowledge and authority by working miracles. To have refused to be baptized as they required, was to disobey God *wilfully*, and show a determination not to be governed by divine commands. That such ought to be debarred from the communion there is no doubt. For this, free communionists have ample provision. But what is the state of the case now? It is very different. Ministers are now, like other men, dependent on the Bible for all their knowledge of divine things. Hence after doing their best to ascertain what the will of the Lord is, they differ as also do the people; at best, they only *believe*, whereas the apostles *knew*.

"One believes immersion is the only mode of baptism, another believes in sprinkling. Both have read and studied the Bible, watched and prayed, to know the truth, and are equally sincere and honest. Their earnest desire is to do the whole will of God. And God owns and blesses one equally with the other. Now admitting that the apostles, having definite knowledge on the subject, did refuse the communion to those who *would not be baptized*, does it follow that ministers, or people, at the present time, who at least but *believe*, are authorized to refuse the communion to those who are equally good with themselves, but happen to differ from them on a disputed point? (one, too, of which they have no positive knowledge.) No reasonable man, who is not blinded either by bigotry or prejudice, can believe it. Thus Mr. K.'s argument from apostolic example falls to the ground, and it being the only one deduced worthy of consideration, his main proposition falls with it.

"Apparently fearing for his cause, after all,

Mr. K. makes another attempt at its defence, more singular than any which has gone before. He says, that, 'when Christ took the twelve apostles into an upper room and brake the bread to them, there were many other true Christians in Jerusalem, who were not invited to participate with them, because not regularly admitted into the church.'

"It may be thought rude, but it is important for me to inquire of Mr. K. where he obtained this information. That it is revealed in our common Bible, no one will pretend. Whether it is in the new Baptist Bible, from which I understand the word baptize is expunged, and immerse put in its place, or whether it is what is sometimes termed *home-made* scripture, I am utterly at a loss to know. At all events it makes sad work with the gospel. It is said in St. Matthew, that all Jerusalem went out and '*were baptized* of John in Jordan.' Is it not strange that no more of them happened to be in Jerusalem at that time? But I will not dwell here. The young convert ought not to be influenced by *assertions*, unless accompanied with proof. The declaration, that 'God does require in his word that all persons should be baptized before they come to the communion table,' is equally unfounded. Where, it may be asked, is the requisition recorded? Or when did the primitive church comply with any such requisition? We have demanded the record, but it has not yet appeared. The truth is, the idea that because a man has neglected baptism we must not allow him to remember his Saviour, is absurd. What would be said should we teach that because a man had neglected to watch, therefore he must not pray? While this theory commands conformity to what is *thought* to have been apostolic example, it *compels* disobedience to the (known) command of Christ, 'Do this in remembrance of me.' Thus, while it accuses us of sin in the one case, it demands that we sin in the other also."—*Porter's Review of Elder Knapp.*

CHAPTER VI.

OPPORTUNITIES FOR SPIRITUAL CULTURE AND FOR USEFULNESS.

The second fact that we were to consider is, the opportunity afforded for spiritual profiting, or growth in grace, by the church of my choice. I find in the Methodist church all those means of grace which are common to other branches of Christ's church ; and several others peculiar to Methodism, such as class-meetings, love-feasts, &c.

Class-meetings are eminently calculated to revive and improve the spirituality, and strengthen the faith of the Christian. They are also pre-eminently adapted to develope the different gifts and talents in the church, and at the same time strengthen the confidence and improve the ability of all. It is there the inexperienced learn wisdom, and the experienced become wiser. There the weak become strong, and the strong renew their strength. It is there the tempted find deliverance, and the delivered become established. There the indifferent are made to feel their responsibility, and those feeling it are moved to action. The timid are encouraged, and the self-confident humbled. In short, every advantage which can result from a friendly Christian intercourse among believers, in holy conference and communion with each other and with their common Lord, is secured in the class-room. Who has not felt the importance of such a privilege to obtain light and instruction, and receive lessons for their own profit in listening to the experience of others? We were made to bless each other in a thousand ways; and we are influenced by the experience as well as example of other Christians.

Class-meetings are a perfect copy of the example of those who, in the days of Malachi, the Prophet, "feared the Lord, and spake often one to another, and the Lord hearkened and heard it, and a book of remembrance was written," &c. "If you are *sincere*, the class-meeting will neither be dreaded nor disliked. There is, perhaps, no religious ordinance more delightful and salutary in its influence on the minds of those who diligently seek God, and who endeavor faithfully to serve him. As they have no motive for concealing their actual state and character, they can sustain the test to which the class-meeting subjects them. They can, with frankness, humility and gratitude, describe their religious experience; and in the utterance of their own feelings, in listening to the statements of their fellow-members, and in receiving the admonitions of their leader, they find themselves stimulated, strengthened, and encouraged; they are blessed with the manifestations of the divine presence and favor, and return to their homes cleaving unto the Lord with increased confidence, attachment, and devotedness. Such are the advantages which class-meetings are the means of conferring on those who resort to them in *sincerity*. But to the unwatchful, cold-hearted, and worldly professor class-meetings are an unwelcome ordeal. His false pretensions, his superficial experience, shrink from the searching investigation." And while a few have shown a lamentable spirit of bigotry and malice toward this institution, merely because it was found among the Methodists, (as in the case of the author of "The Great Iron Wheel," of whom it was fitly said by one of his own denominational brethren, that "his faith evidently worked by *malice* instead of *love*,") a much larger portion of other denominations generously and frankly admit the fitness and wisdom of this means of grace. An influential member of the Congregational church, who was strongly attached to that people, and had been as strongly opposed to the Methodists until an acquaintance with them removed his prejudices, said to me, "I admire your social meetings, especially your class-meetings; by that means you become acquainted with each other's spiritual state, which not only prepares you to sympathize with, and labor for, each other, but also cultivates bretherly love, and affords an opportunity to encourage and 'exhort one another,' as the Bible commands." And said he, "I tell my brethren that we greatly need some such social means of grace, for we know nothing of the spiritual state of the members of the church, except that we see them at church and the communion; and how can we labor together; it is impossible."

Love-feasts are of less frequent occurrence, generally connected with Quarterly Meetings, and are composed of all the members in the society or circuit, as far as it is convenient for them to meet on the occasion. The nature of the meeting is similar to class-meetings, though different in some respects. Those present on these occasions, partake of bread and water, in token of their love and friendship, and then speak freely of their present or past experience, as they may be led by the Spirit's influence. This means of grace is much loved by all genuine Methodists; and it is a service of peculiar interest and profit to the young convert, and a season of great refreshing to the whole church; "a feast of fat things, of wine on the lees well refined," a blessed foretaste of Heaven above. Many are the testimonials which have been received in favor of this institution from members of other churches, who have been present at these *feasts of love.* Said a venerable man and an influential deacon in a sister church, previous to going to a love-feast, with his friends who were Methodists, "I think you would do well to change the name of your meeting; the design is undoubtedly a good one, but some object to the name 'Love-Feast,' as not a Scriptural one." But after he had witnessed the exercise, and partook of the spirit of love and holy joy that prevailed, as he came out of the meeting he said, "I will recall my suggestion to alter the name of your meeting; I am satisfied now you could not get a more appropriate one; you do well to call it a Love-Feast, for so it is in reality." Then there is something peculiar in Methodist prayer-meetings. Not only that they are held more frequently than among most other denominations, but there is a degree of *spirit*, *life*, and ENERGY in them, found in no other. This is attributable to two causes, viz.: their faith or sentiment, and the advantages of class meetings. They believe that the Christian life is one of constant, *vigorous action*. So they understand the Scriptures to teach. Paul cries to the armies of God's Israel, "Fight the good fight of faith," "run the race." They listen again, and they hear the Great Captain of our salvation saying, "Strive to enter in at the strait gate." "Work while the day lasts." "Be zealous." And again James encourages them with the assurance that, "the effectual *fervent* prayer of a righteous man availeth much." In view of these and a countless number of similar Scriptures, they believe it the duty of every Christian to stand as a bold witness for God and his cause, a valiant *active* soldier of Christ. They believe also that it is the Christian's privilege to "be joyful in the house of prayer," as well as deeply earnest in their supplications in behalf of the world's conversion; to enjoy such a measure of the divine presence and power as to fill the soul with holy comfort, perfect peace, and joy unspeakable. "According to thy faith, so be it unto thee." Hence the great and lamented Dr. Chalmers, a Presbyterian, was led to exclaim, "Methodism is Christianity in earnest."

Then they have become accustomed to bearing the cross in their class-meetings, where there were none to criticise, but all to pray; hence the ready and cheerful manner in which they bear testimony for God, both in prayer and exhortation; and "God loveth the cheerful giver." It is here you find that *solemn* earnestness combined with cheerful holy delight, which is found no where else. In addition to these privileges, the plain, practical, extemporaneous, and pointed manner of preaching among Methodists is much better calculated to reach the heart and improve the spirituality, than the written essays which too often take the place of preaching.

The third and last question is, Where can I do the most good? What church is best adapted to fulfil the great commission, "Go ye into all the world and preach the gospel to every creature," to convert the world?

That is the best system of church polity, which, while it conforms to the Bible in all things therein defined, affords the greatest advantages for doing good, both to its own members and to the world at large. The great distinguishing feature of Methodist polity is her system of an itinerant ministry, in connection with extemporaneous preaching. To an itinerant ministry many object, not because it is not useful, but because it is unpleasant, requires great sacrifice and self-denial, &c. But the object of the ministry is to *save men*, not to gratify their wishes or please their tastes, only so far as they accord with the best interests of Christ's cause. *Benevolence*, not selfishness, is the appropriate principle of action in the ministry as well as in all religion. We are bound to support that system which is most efficient in securing the objects of the ministry. This is very generally overlooked, and the fact that nearly every objection brought against the itinerancy is based on the principle of selfishness, is a strong argument in its favor: for instance, as the oft repeated expression, "when we get a good minister we want to keep him!" Now he is not your minister, but God's minister to the world, and he belongs to the world; and if you have been favored with an able and successful minister two years, why not be willing others should have the same privilege? But "we pay a large salary, and we must have a talented (or smart) man." How perfectly selfish! "But it is so unpleasant to leave one's friends, to move so often," &c. Who, then, would go to carry the gospel to the heathen? When would the Saviour have left the Father's throne to come to earth, if he had waited till it was a pleasant task? Besides, it is much pleasanter to leave those we love, than to be driven away by those who hate us. But it affords too short a time to become acquainted with the people, — is another popular objection. A short time only will be found necessary for a faithful pastor to become sufficiently acquainted for all practical purposes connected with his ministry, and any farther acquaintance is not only unnecessary, but a decided disadvantage. A too familiar acquaintance with all the matters in the community is a great embarrassment to the preacher of the Gospel. But it is said, "the pastoral relation should be permanent." But it should be remembered that Methodist churches are *never* without a pastor, nor the minister without a charge. Whereas all other churches are frequently left "destitute" for a long time, and are always liable to be; the same is true of their ministers. While the Methodist itinerancy secures to every church a pastor and to every pastor a charge, so that the term "destitute" is not known among them, except in cases of death or suspension from the ministry — and then they are sure to be at once supplied.

But is an itinerating ministry Scriptural, and is it the most efficient? These are the only proper questions. That it is Scriptural is evident from the following Scriptural facts. Christ was himself an itinerant. He "*went about* doing good," from town to town, and from city to city;" preaching in the country waste, and in the city full. Matthew says, "He went about all Galilee, teaching in their synagogues, and preaching the gospel of the kingdom." "He went about all the cities and villages." Neither the unbelief and persecutions of his enemies could prevent his giving them the offer of life, nor the affection or flattery of his friends detain him, or prevent his leaving them to go and preach to others. And when he called Peter and Andrew his brother to the ministry, he said, "Follow me, and I will make you fishers of men." And they did so; so of the other disciples. "They followed him." When he sent out the twelve to preach, he said to them, "*As ye go, preach*, saying the kingdom of heaven is at hand." The history of the labors of the apostles is a demonstration of their itinerating character. The *travels* of St. Paul are proverbial. Three years is the longest time we have any account of their ever stopping in one place.

Nothing is more evident from the Scriptures than that the apostles were itinerant ministers.

That it is more efficient than a settled ministry, is also evident from the following considerations:

Men are differently constituted; and they probably differ more mentally and morally than than they do physically. Some have logical, reasoning minds, and no preaching interests or benefits them but the argumentative. Sermons made up of sound, logical argument, are the only sermons for them. Let Paul reason of righteousness, temperance, and a judgment to come, and their minds are interested and their hearts moved. Others seem never to reason logically or to take any interest in such preaching; they want plain, pointed, matter of fact preaching, that comes warm from the heart, and with power. Let Peter utter his thunders and they are pleased and profited. While others are charmed by the chaste and eloquent strains of Apollos. Others again have a mind very susceptible of the plaintive and the sympathetic; with them it is all the same whether Paul reasons, Peter thunders, or Apollos charms; but let the son of consolation or the loving John pour forth his pathetic strains, and they cry, "I yield, I yield; I can hold out no more." While to others it would be like pouring water on a rock; it might wear it, but never break it; nothing but the *fire* and the hammer will do that. And the Lord chooses his ministers in view of these facts. Hence we find not only in the days of the apostles, but in every age, men of all these different constitutional peculiarities and tastes in the ministry; men with gifts and grades of talent adapted to all the different minds in the world. We find more or less of all these different classes in every community, consequently in every congregation the itinerancy is perfectly adapted to meet this state of things. This year they have a successor of Paul with his logical sermons, and an important class of minds are especially benefited, the unbelieving converted, and the saints built up. He is removed and is followed by a plain, matter of fact, hortatory preacher, who, Boanerges-like, utters his thunders in their ears, and another class are reached, gathered into the church, and built up in the faith. He is followed by an eloquent Apollos, a loving John, or a weeping Barnabas, and so all the different classes are blessed with a minister whose gift is adapted to their peculiar character. Whereas on the principle of a settled ministry only one class of minds would be especially profited, and the remainder, though they "liked what the minister said well enough," yet they would feel no very great interest in it, and would not be materially benefited. To say that every minister should possess all these gifts, is to say that they should be more perfect than the apostles. That these are important truths, and not mere speculations, is evident from the history of the church in all ages. Where will you look for as frequent revivals of religion as are seen among itinerant ministers? The great proportion of revivals among the settled ministry have been through the labors of itinerating evangelists; yet, including these, they have been very few when compared with the number among the regular Methodist itinerants, as the history of the church plainly shows. Said a deacon of one of the oldest as well as one of the most influential Congregational churches in his county, "I have been a member of our church ever since its organization. We have had so many ministers; some for one year, and others for a number of years in succession, and in every instance of a change of ministers we have been blessed with some revival, but none of them have ever been favored with but one season of revival while with us;" — and, said he, "I have thought of it much, why it was so." The mystery is easily solved by the preceding statements. This accounts also for the frequent removals, where men are settled for an indefinite number of years, or hired from year to year; for recently they move about as often on the whole as Methodists; but while we move by system they move by constraint, or from necessity, (for it would be uncharitable to suppose that it is to obtain larger salaries.) The fact is, that unless one class of minds have the controlling influence, a portion of the hearers to whom the preaching, though ever so good, is not adapted, will, after two or three years at most, become dissatisfied, and want a change, and either the minister will ask a dismission to prevent what is worse, and go out to hunt up another field, leaving the church "destitute," or he will remain, and discord and division will be the consequence. Dislike it as we may, it is impossible for one minisier to suit every body; and yet all classes of men are represented in almost every community.

The defence of the gospel is an important work, but one for which many good ministers have little taste or capacity. Yet error is wide-spread over the earth, and God has called some logical clear-sighted men, who, like Paul, are able to analyze error, and undermine its foundations, exposing the sophistical reasoning of its advocates. But how shall the comparatively few who are blessed with this gift perform this work, unless they itinerate as did the great Apostle? Some ministers have a peculiar ability to explain the doctrines and institutions of the church; enforcing their obligations, while others have not that gift. But every church needs to have them explained and enforced.

2. The itinerancy has a powerful influence on the ministry to preserve its purity and piety. In view of the apparent ease, honor, and wealth connected with a settled ministry with large salaries, there is some inducement for men to

choose the office from worldly motives, and also tendencies to backsliding, by fostering pride or love of the world in those who have entered the ministry from better motives. But such are the sacrifices of an itinerant minister, both of ease and the prospect of worldly gain, that no man would ever enter its ranks unless he felt as did Paul, that "woe is me if I preach not the gospel;" unless it was through a mistaken idea, and then he would very soon find it convenient to leave for some other field. The labor and sacrifice also, connected with it, tends to keep them humble, and drive them to a throne of grace for help.

3. It avoids the temptation to preach to please the people, so necessarily connected with preaching as candidates for a "call," (a most unpleasant task certainly,) and it enables their minister to speak the truth fearlessly, as he does not see the rod of dismission held over his head, to be let fall if his plain and pointed manner should offend some sinner in or out of the church.

4. It has the advantage of a natural love of novelty. Disguise it as we may, men do love

new things. It is true of all men; and many will be attracted to the house of God by the charm of a new minister, who would not go to hear the old one, be he ever so able. And if men are to be saved by the foolishness of preaching, they must be induced to hear it.

5. It supplies a large number of feeble societies with constant preaching, which could never be supplied on the principle of a settled ministry. A preacher is sent them this year, and they pay him what little they can, and he by economy lives through the year, and perhaps two, and then goes to an abler appointment and another takes his place. Thus thousands of feeble societies are supplied until God adds to their strength. Or a number of these feeble societies are joined together, forming a circuit, including many destitute places where there are no societies. This circuit is travelled by one or more preachers, who visit the several places at stated intervals, not only supplying the feeble but also carrying the gospel where there are no religious privileges. In this way Methodism has supplied the frontier of the great West for fifty years, by which means a pure religion has been

able to keep pace with emigration in that important field. In this way nine tenths of the Methodist churches have been built up. The preacher has gone uncalled, and called the people; some have obeyed the call; a society has been formed, and finally a church erected, and the gospel with its institutions established. It has been fitly said, that "the usual stationary ministry *waits for the call of the people, while the Methodist ministry goes forth to call the people.* This is one of its strongest points of contrast. Christianity is essentially missionary in its character; unlike Judaism, local and confined to one nation, it is aggressive, and takes in the world. To this character agrees the system of Methodist itinerancy. It is calculated to encompass the world with one band of itinerant missionaries; for every Methodist itinerant is a missionary, either *home* or *foreign*. Indeed, the Methodist Church is one great missionary society, sending out her missionaries to preach the gospel to the poor and destitute at home, and to the heathen abroad. It is her glory that by her means, more than every other, "*the poor have the gospel preached to them.*" The fact that she includes within her pale a larger portion of the poor in this world's goods, both in Europe and America, than any other church, has been considered by some as a reproach; but such should remember that our Saviour included the fact that "the poor have the gospel preached to them," among the proofs of his Messiahship. Thus speaks Rev. Abel Stevens on this subject: "Much of what was our frontier, but since has become the most important states of the Union, would have passed through the forming period of its character destitute, to a great extent, of the influence of Christian institutions. But the Methodist itinerancy has borne the cross, not only in the midst, but in the van of the hosts of emigration. Methodist itinerants are found with their horses and saddle-bags, threading the trail of the savage, cheering and blessing with their visits the loneliest cottage on the farthest frontier. They have gone to aboriginal tribes, and have gathered into the pale of the church more of the children of the forest than any other sect; they have scaled the Rocky Mountains, and are building up Christianity and civilization on the shores of the Columbia; they are hastening down towards the capitol of Montezuma, (which they have now reached,) while, throughout the length and breadth of our older states, they have been spreading a healthful influence which has affected all classes, so that their cause includes not only a larger aggregate population than any other sect, but, especially, a larger proportion of those classes whose moral elevation is the most difficult and the most important." Dr. Baird, (a Presbyterian) in his late invaluable work on Religion in America, speaking of difficult portions of our moral field, exclaims, "Blessed be God, there is a way, as I shall show hereafter, by which some of the evils here spoken of may be mitigated, and that is by the system of itinerant preaching employed so extensively and usefully by the Methodists." And again he says: "It has been said with truth, that the Methodist church is in its very structure emphatically missionary, and it is an inexpressible blessing that it is so, as the United States strikingly prove. The whole country is embraced in one General Conference; it is again subdivided into annual conferences, each including a large extent of territory, and divided into districts. Each district comprehends several circuits, (and stations,) and within each circuit there are from five or six to above twenty preaching places." He then describes the manner in which the circuit preacher visits and conducts regular service in each of these places, either in "a church, school-room, or dwelling house," on the Sabbath in the larger places, and on a week day, or evening, in others. He adds, "Thus the gospel is carried into thousands of remote spots, in which it never would be preached upon the plan of having a permanent clergy, planted in particular districts and parishes." It was a remark, I believe, of the celebrated Dr. Witherspoon, that "he needed no other evidence that the Rev. John Wesley was a great man, than what the system of itinerating preaching presented to his mind, and of which that wonderful man was the author." The observation was a just one. It is a system of vast importance in every point of view, capable of being made to send its ramifications into almost every corner of the country, and to carry the glad tidings of salvation into the most remote and secluded settlements, as well as to the more accessible and populous towns and neighborhoods."

6. It avoids all those difficulties which naturally, if not necessarily, grow out of the practice of settling ministers for an indefinite number of years. As a very natural result, one part of the society will become dissatisfied, and call for a change, and begin to agitate the matter; this excites those of an opposite opinion, and they become aroused, and division of the society in feeling, and often in fact, takes place. If the minister remains, his usefulness is at an end, and if he goes, it will be almost certain that his successor will not please his particular friends; and so the church is rent, and the cause of Christ is wounded in the house of his friends. But not unfrequently the minister becomes one of the party, and a prosecution perhaps is the result, and in some instances as many as half a dozen lawsuits have resulted from an effort to dismiss a settled minister. There is scarcely a society of long standing among the settled order, but has seen more or less of these troubles, and not a few have been nearly or quite ruined by them. The ecclesiastical history of New England is

full of these minister and society controversies. The practice of hiring by the year is but little less liable to these difficulties. It leaves the minister in constant suspense as to the time of his stay, being liable to dismissal at the end of every year, with no place to which he can go until he has time to find one, and in cases of removal, which are frequent when left at the option of the people, some months will ordinarily intervene before he will find another location, or the church he left another pastor. He and his family are all the time on expense, and the church is destitute. Nothing is more common in looking over the minutes of their associations, than to see a large number of churches marked "destitute." We do not wonder that they are becoming weary of this kind of itinerancy, for it possesses all the disadvantages with an insupportable addition, and scarcely any of the advantages of our system. I was interested in reading the pastoral address of two Baptist associations to their members, urging several reasons against so frequent removals, most of which were really valid objections, and applicable to their way of doing it, but had not the least bearing upon our systematic itinerancy. We will conclude this topic with a short extract from a distinguished writer in the "Encyclopædia of Religious Knowledge," and one of the settled order. He says: "Notwithstanding the prejudices of mankind, and the indiscretions of some individuals, an *itinerant teacher* is one of the most honorable and useful characters to be found upon earth; and there needs no other proof than the experience of the church in all ages, that where this work is done properly and with perseverance, it forms the grand method of spreading wide, and rendering efficacious, religious knowledge; for great reformations and revivals of religion have uniformly been thus affected; and it has been especially sanctioned by the *example* of *Christ* and his apostles, and recommended as the *divine method* of spreading the gospel through the nations of the earth."

Intimately connected with the Methodist itinerancy is the practice of extemporaneous preaching. While nearly all others at the present day are in the habit of reading sermons, Methodist ministers preach them. In this respect at least, they are in the true "Apostolical succession," or in the practice of the course pursued by the Saviour and his apostles, as well as the whole primitive church, in which such an anomaly as reading sermons was not known. But Methodists do not justify it on this ground merely, but because it is the more effectual mode of preaching; not but that men do good that read their sermons, but who ever heard of a man who was wholly confined to his notes, having a powerful revival of religion under his preaching? The fact that all denominations who make special efforts for revivals lay aside their note books at such times, and address themselves direct to the people, shows that reading sermons, though it may enable the minister to exhibit his talent as a writer, and to please and astonish the hearer, yet it does not "convert the sinner from the error of his way." Few souls, comparatively, we apprehend, were ever brought to Christ by hearing sermons read, though we do not doubt but some have, as others have been by reading good books at home.

Rev. J. Porter, in his recent and deservedly popular work on revivals, says: "Preaching should be *extempore.* If the business of the ministry was only to announce the truth, the case would be different. But an effect is to be secured which requires the soul's deepest sympathy, and the fullest manifestation of it, in treating with sinners; a sympathy arising from Christian affection, and aroused by the present discovery of the ruinous results of continued impenitence, rather than by reading the conceptions of other days, and perhaps of other minds. It is not enough for the hearer to see his minister weeping over the touching language of a studied manuscript, written he knows not when! He wishes to hear him speak in the expressive language of his present emotions. There is always a sort of distrust connected with the sight of a manuscript, chilling to the sensibilities. Besides, it is impossible for a minister to read with as much *emphasis* and power as he may speak. He needs to *see* his hearers, and have them see him. The maker of the 'human face divine,' gave a tongue to every feature. Reading deranges the whole, so that no one speaks naturally. There is power also in gesture, but reading destroys it. In fact it mars the whole performance. The heart is comparatively stupified, the hands tied, the feet fettered, the body often transfixed, and every expression of the countenance perverted. Extemporary preaching has equal advantage as a mode of instruction. By universal consent and approval, professors and teachers generally extemporize. Readers, if such an anomaly were to appear, would find no patronage. Parents wish their children to be taken under close and familiar tuition, and holden to the work till they are compelled to understand. The children of God, and sinners too, need a similar training. But why do not the judge and the advocate read? What would a client say, even a sermon-reading minister, were his lawyer to read a plea? Would he be pleased with the idea? Is it not nearly certain that such a lawyer would get no business? Or why is it that sermon-reading ministers often lay aside their notes in times of revival? The answer is one — extemporary speaking is the more effective. So we believe, and so we teach, and the history of preaching sustains us in our position.

"But aside from all these considerations, extemporary preaching was the model style Jesus Christ we think was never suspected of preaching a written sermon. He spake from other influences than that of a manuscript. The message was in his *heart* and mind, and he preached from the intensity of his love for a perishing world. And so did the apostles, who testified of his resurrection. Reading sermons is a modern invention, owing its origin to political jealousy. With that jealousy it should have passed away into everlasting disuse."

CHAPTER VII.

FRUITS OF METHODISM.

In concluding this subject we will notice briefly some of the fruits of Methodism; for our Saviour has told us that, "by their fruits ye shall know them." Let us apply this rule to the history and present state of the Methodist church in comparison with other churches. Methodism had its beginning as an organization in England, and is known there by the name of Wesleyan Methodism. It commenced but about one hundred years ago; yet there are now 16,226 preachers, travelling and local; 459,454 members; equalling in numbers all the other dissenting churches. But their usefulness is seen still more in their missionary operations. They have 295 missionary stations, 417 missionaries, with 106,445 members. The amount raised by them last year for missions was $508,800. Then there are 100,000 of other Methodist bodies not reckoned in the above number. Methodism is much younger in England than most of the other dissenting churches, yet now she outnumbers them all counted together, and excels them all in the missionary work. May we not learn something from these facts in reference to her advantages for doing good? Also with reference to the estimation in which she is held by the Great Head of the church?

But how is it in this country? Methodism has existed here as an organized body a little more than sixty years; and including the different branches of the Methodist family, who all hold the same faith, they now number 1,243,649 members. The northern portion of the Methodist Episcopal church has seven colleges, thirty-eight seminaries, and one Theological or Biblical Institution. The Baptist denomination is more than one hundred years older in this country, and claims to be the only people who obey God, in keeping the ordinances as he requires, and in reality the only church in existence, — as baptism, they say, is the only door into the church, and they are the only consistent baptized believers; yet, including all the different denominations of Baptists, a large portion of whom hold nothing in common, except immersion, they have 921,073 members, about 300,000 less than the Methodists; while in England they are less than half their number. The Congregationalist church, whose history is as old as the country, possessing every earthly advantage, has a little short of 200,000 members, not quite one sixth as many as the Methodist. The Protestant Episcopal church, which arrogates to itself the title of "*the* church," in the most exclusive sense, has 72,099 members; about one-seventeenth of the number of the Methodist. Surely, whom doth the Lord delight to honor? We have made these comparisons simply to show the great efficiency of Methodism, and for no other purpose. And what do we see? We see a denomination commencing long after the field was occupied by others, and contending at every step with the popular feeling in favor of previously existing churches, and the strong prejudices of the people against its doctrines and usages. Most of its members are poor in this world's goods, its ministry is for the most part unlearned in the wisdom of the schools, yet in about fifty years it outnumbers all. But, is it said great increase of numbers is no proof of great usefulness? We admit that it is not where evidence of piety is not made a test of membership; but who will say that the members of the Methodist church are not as uniformly pious as any other denomination? No candid man will say this: for it is not true. Therefore, in this and all similar cases, increase of numbers during a series of years is a proper test of usefulness. But not where people are converted by force of arms, or received into the church without being made any better, as in the case of the Romanists.

"Had Methodists been *rich* in this world's goods, their success might have been attributed to this cause; but like the Saviour and his early disciples, they have generally been poor. They could not appeal to the pride and vanity of the world by erecting splendid churches, and otherwise making a great display, if they were disposed. They have had to preach in private dwellings, school-houses, barns, and in the open air, till they could erect churches. And many of these, for the want of means, have had to be small, and often out of place and uninviting. And the world has looked on and mocked, and professors of religion have not unfrequently joined in the sport. This same cause has been an occasion of reproach to preachers, who have often had to live in a style directly calculated to lessen the respect of community for them, and also for their enterprise. But God has prospered their work, nevertheless, and their word has been with power.

"Yes, in spite of all these disadvantages — in the face of popular scorn — of open and violent persecution — of oppressive legislation, and of a regular settled ministry, they have been able to outstrip all other sects, and to stand first in numbers and in efficiency, in converting sinners to God, which is the principal work of the church and ministry, and the proper test of their usefulness."

The following tribute to the Methodist Episcopal church, from the pen of Dr. Baird, a Presbyterian, was written before the separation of the Southern Conferences.

"Since its organization in 1784, though not

without its share of difficulties, its career, upon the whole, has been remarkably prosperous, and God has enabled it to overcome every hindrance with wonderful success. We have seen the numerical amount of its members sixty years ago, to be 15,000; in 1843, it was 1,068,525 communicants. And the probable proportion of the community under the influence of this church's ministry, is 5,000,000. Surely we may well exclaim, 'What hath God wrought!' It covers the whole land with its net-work system of stations and circuits, and carries the gospel into thousands of the most remote as well as the most secluded and thinly peopled neighborhoods. This denomination has made great exertions to increase the number of its church edifices within the last few years. But its itinerating ministers preach in thousands of places where no such buildings are yet erected, or at least none belonging to that denomination. In these cases they hold their meetings in school houses, court houses, and private houses. No American Christian who takes a comprehensive view of the progress of religion in this country, and considers how wonderfully the means and instrumentalities employed are adapted to the wants of that country, can hesitate for a moment to bless God for having, in his mercy, provided them all. Nor will he fail to recognize in the Methodist economy, as well as in the zeal, the devoted piety, and the efficiency of its ministry, one of the most powerful elements in the religious prosperity of the United States, *as well as one of the firmest pillars of their civil and political institutions.*"

"But this is only a partial view of the success of Methodism. We must look to the records of other churches if we will have any adequate conception of what it has done. There are thousands and tens of thousands among them who were awakened and converted through the instrumentality of Methodists. Many things have contributed to draw them away from their spiritual relations, and they have settled down in church fellowship with those who never 'travailed in birth' for them.*

* For however much they may complain of "noisy Methodist meetings," or be shocked at their 'excitement and want of order," they are ever ready to receive the fruits of revivals among Methodists, making no objection to the convert's "hope," though it was obtained at a camp-meeting.

"But these churches have been more especially benefited by Methodism in another way. It has 'provoked' them to love and good works. Their ministers are better preachers, better pastors, and better Christians — they have more zeal and enterprize — preach less error and more truth, and otherwise labor more appropriately than when Methodism was first introduced among them. And their people have improved in the same ratio. Where the family altar was entirely neglected, it now smokes with acceptable incense. Where there were but two meetings in a week, and those in the parish church, there are now several, in various places, to accommodate the people. Where there were pride and worldly amusement, with little piety and enterprise, there are now to be found Christian activity and devotion to God. Such has been the effect of Methodism upon them, that churches which feared and trembled at the approach of the itinerant, have become firmer, more united and spiritual than they ever were before, and have reason to bless God for the Providence which brought so useful an agency among them. Had we not succeeded in forming a single church, or in doing any other good, the influence we have exerted on surrounding denominations is an abundant compensation for all our sacrifices." Such are some of the fruits of Methodism.

We have now given our principal reasons for becoming a Methodist. It was not, therefore, because we consider the Methodist Episcopal church the only true or Christian church. We had become fully satisfied that there was no one of the different churches which could with the least propriety claim to be "the church," in that exclusive sense in which this phrase is used by Episcopalians, and no less claimed by the principles of the Baptist church in regard to baptism and the communion, for this would imply an exclusive right to the Divine blessing. Nothing is more manifest than that no one church can, without making themselves ridiculous in the eyes of all sober men, lay any claim to such exclusive honor; much less those who are far behind their neighbors in usefulness. The most that can be said of any church in this respect is, that its doctrines are freer from error, that its economy is better adapted to strengthen the Christian in the graces of the spirit, convert sinners from the error of their ways, and that greater success has attended its labors, more sinners having been saved through its instrumentality. This we think we have shown to be true of Methodism. Let the reader judge. I found much to admire and love in the Congregationalist church — the evangelical character of her doctrines, the manifest piety of her members, their zeal and liberality in supporting the benevolent institutions of the church, as well as the truly Catholic spirit which at the present day quite generally prevails among both her ministry and membership. For these noble, praiseworthy, and most important traits of character I respect and love her, and rejoice to be found laboring in fellowship with such a people. But not believing in the doctrines of Calvinism, and finding them, on examination, interwoven with every part of her system of theology, I could not believe it my duty to seek a home within her pale, and thereby adopt her sentiments, and place myself under an obligation to defend them, especially when the Methodist church afforded me all these advantages and even more, and was perfectly free from the influence of Calvinism.

The Calvinist Baptist church I respect and love for her evangelical character. I admire her zeal in laboring to convert sinners at home, and to carry the gospel to the heathen abroad. But as she is equally Calvinistic with Congregationalists and Presbyterians, I could not consistently embrace her doctrines — much less adopt her exclusive and bigoted sentiments in regard to baptism and the communion. And there is a strong resemblance between her sentiments on this subject and the unfounded and ridiculous pretensions of Episcopalians to "Apostolical succession." This was strikingly illustrated by the following circumstance. Two young men, class-mates in college, both entered the ministry. One became an Episcopalian, the other a Close-Communion Baptist. The Episcopalian, on a visit to his old class-mate, spent the Sabbath with him, and preached for him in the morning; — during recess the Baptist brother seemed quite troubled about something, and just before the commencement of the service he remarked, "Brother, we were highly pleased with your sermon, but I am sorry it happens so, we have our communion this afternoon, and I really wish we could invite you to commune with us, but you know we don't think you have been baptized, and so I suppose we could not do it." "Very well," replied the Episcopalian, "I could not receive the sacrament at your hands, for I don't think you have been ordained."

This striking similarity between their views and the intolerant claims of the Episcopal church, has led the Baptists in England to give up their close communion in very many places, and many of her ablest men have renounced it altogether; and although the Baptists here seem to cling the closer to their intolerant principles, yet we believe the time will come when such an anomaly as close communion will not be known; when all God's family will sit down at the same table, when "Ephraim shall not envy Judah, and Judah shall not vex Ephraim." But so long as these intolerant claims are held by Episcopalians and Baptists, so long will that proselyting and uncharitable spirit which is now so frequently witnessed, (and greatly to the disadvantage of pure religion,) be seen as the natural and almost necessary fruits of these exclusive principles. But, says Mr. Remington, "The practice of close communion does not lead to bigotry; if it did, the Baptists would have been persecutors." But he should remember that the spirit of persecution is often seen in other forms than in imprisonments, racks, and tortures, and that it will be quite in time for Baptists to boast in this matter when they have once had the whip in their hands and refused to use it. He would do well also to remember the saying of their great apostle, Robert Hall, viz.: That their views of the communion *were equally intolerant* with the bigoted principles of Romanism, that the one was "the intolerance of power, the other of weakness." That they do lead to bigotry, he (Mr. Remington) has himself shown, as any one may see by reading his two pamphlets, the first, "Reasons for Becoming a Baptist," written when he had just embraced these *sentiments*; the other, "Defence of Restricted Communion," when he had not only embraced the theory, but the *spirit* also, the fruits of which are seen in the gross perversions and misrepresentations of the discipline of a church to which he owed, under God, the salvation of his soul.

In conclusion we remark, that although it was at a sacrifice of worldly influence, or popularity, that we joined the Methodist church, yet we bless the day when we entered its pale. The longer we live in the church, and the more we see of its true character and usefulness, the more we admire, love, and venerate it. May God preserve her primitive simplicity of doctrine, the wisdom of her economy, and the deep piety and earnest burning zeal of her ministry and membership.

THE END.

www.ingramcontent.com/pod-product-compliance
Lightning Source LLC
LaVergne TN
LVHW021403110826
845150LV00007B/1770

* 9 7 8 1 4 2 5 5 1 2 5 9 0 *